A Guide to Writing Papers

Third edition

Edward J. Martin
Columbus State Community College

McGraw-Hill, Inc.
College Custom Series

New York   St. Louis   San Francisco   Auckland   Bogotá
Caracas   Lisbon   London   Madrid   Mexico   Milan   Montreal
New Delhi   Paris   San Juan   Singapore   Sydney   Tokyo   Toronto

McGraw-Hill's **College Custom Series** consists of products that are produced from camera-ready copy. Peer review, class testing, and accuracy are primarily the responsibility of the author(s).

A GUIDE TO WRITING PAPERS

7 8 9 0 BBC BBC 9 0 9 8

ISBN 0-07-040842-4

Editor: Jan Scipio

Cover Design: Kira Sholeen

Printer/Binder: Braceland,Inc.

 This book is printed on recycled paper containing 10% postconsumer waste.

CONTENTS

iv

ACKNOWLEDGMENTS

I am indebted to many people for helping me prepare this book. The staff members of the Educational Resources Center have been most helpful. Students have freely permitted me to adapt and use their work as examples and exercises. And my colleagues have willingly shared their materials as well as their critical insights. For their help I am very thankful.

A special word of thanks is due to the many faculty members in the Communication Skills Department who have read and commented on the many drafts of this book. In particular I would like to thank Robert Boyer, Elizabeth Copley, Jack Tabor, Barbara Thompson, Phyllis Prater, Lynn Turnipseed, and my office mate Donald Ehret. Their critical observations and editorial assistance have greatly improved this book.

For their help on the graphic elements of this book, I wish to thank Nancy Cleland (Public Relations); Connie Faddis (Academic Affairs); Jane Goostree and Ann Fields (Educational Resources Center).

Perhaps the most important part of the book was written not by me but by Sandra Theis who generated the index. I will think of her whenever I use it.

Finally, I want to thank Kimberly Hawkes, Shelly Reed, and Michele Welsh through whose computer and desk top publishing skills this book took its final shape.

FOREWORD

Welcome to Columbus State Community College.

The administrators, faculty, and staff are glad to be a part of your academic plans. Everyone is committed to giving you the knowledge and skills you will need to be successful in college and on the job.

The college recognizes that your success depends largely on your ability to read critically and to write effectively. That is why you will see reading and writing being emphasized increasingly across the curriculum. In the Communication Skills Department you will learn the basic steps of the writing process as you proceed from simple compositions to research papers. Many courses in the Arts and Sciences Division may also require such assignments as term papers, book reports, critiques, annotated bibliographies, and reaction papers. Your major field will introduce you to the kinds of writing needed to be successful on the job; for example, incident reports and case studies.

It is vital that you understand what is expected from you and have some strategies for completing these tasks if you want to do these assignments successfully. The purpose of this book is to help you understand these assignments better and to give you some strategies for completing them.

This book assumes that you have or will gain in your classes a basic understanding of the library. If not, you should participate in a tour of the Educational Resources Center. These orientations are given many times every quarter, and you are welcome to join one any time it is convenient.

Research Skills

Without discussing in detail all of the library resources, this book outlines a **search strategy** so that the time you spend in the Educational Resources Center or any library will be used efficiently.

Once you have found information, you need a practical and consistent system for extracting, presenting, and documenting the information you find so that you do not commit the serious academic offense of **plagiarism.** This book describes an effective procedure for preparing the research paper, and it explains how to complete the main steps:

1. Bibliography--for preliminary cards and the Works Cited page
2. Note cards
3. Lead-ins and internal documentation
4. Organizational principles and outline models
5. Acceptable manuscript format

Computer applications are discussed where appropriate to the research and writing process.

Sample papers are included for you to see what the finished product might look like. You should consider these papers examples of what can be done, not models that you must slavishly imitate.

In addition to the material on the research paper, you will find general guidelines and examples for documenting literary papers.

I have tried to make this material as complete, helpful, and readable as possible. I hope it contributes to your academic success. If you have questions, comments, or suggestions for future revisions, please direct them to me in the Communication Skills Department.

Edward J. Martin

Communication Skills Department

HOW TO USE THIS GUIDE--
THE PROCESSES OF WRITING AND CONDUCTING RESEARCH

You can approach this writing guide in at least two different ways. First, you can read it cover to cover. This approach takes you methodically through the basic steps in conducting library research: finding a topic, gathering material, preparing a bibliography, organizing a paper, taking notes to flesh out the outline, documenting the material you use in the paper, and preparing the final manuscript.

However, most experienced writers and researchers will tell you that the process does not occur in this neat, step-by-step linear order. Instead, research and writing often proceed by fits and starts; you may often need to jump ahead or fall back a step. Often you may be doing several tasks at the same time: drafting, rechecking sources, and sharing your work with others, for example.

A second approach uses this guide as a resource book that you can turn to as your research needs arise. You may want to start by studying the sample papers to see what a finished product might look like. You will certainly need to return to the section called "The Bibliography" time after time, as you encounter new sources and need to write an appropriate entry.

You should also consider this guide a supplement to rather than a replacement for your English rhetoric or handbook. Those books provide detailed discussions of the writing process and the elements of style. You should consult them when those kinds of questions arise.

Your rhetoric or handbook will provide comprehensive coverage of the processes of conducting research and writing the research paper. It should also include help for the writing you need to do in other courses such as taking essay examinations.

As a supplement, this guide tries to provide the specific insights you will need for conducting research in the Educational Resources Center, and it tries to help you better understand those points that many students have found troublesome in doing research papers. You can see how to avoid these problems and thereby be more successful in completing assignments at Columbus State.

THE RESEARCH PAPER--A DEFINITION

For undergraduates the research paper is a learning tool. By completing the assignment, you gain knowledge about your topic and skills for conducting the research process more effectively. At the outset, you need to consider two questions: (1) What voice should you have in your paper, and (2) What is your role as researcher?

Your Voice as Writer

At the beginning level, a research paper is generally a summary of what others have already said or written on a subject. In writing your research papers, you will typically be using information that is already known, rather than conducting your own experiments and first-hand research. Most of your paper will focus on your topic and, therefore, should be presented objectively in **third person** without writing, "I discovered . . ." or "My research shows . . ."

However, you can certainly draw from your own interests, knowledge, and experience. Traditionally, students have been taught to present this information in the third person. They have been advised to use expressions like the following:

> From an interview with Bobby Rahal **this writer** learned . . .
> **To this researcher**, the logic of the school board's argument seems confused.

These indirect references can sound awkward or pompous. Therefore, the more recent practice is to use first person (I, me, my) when you present your own experiences and observations. But when doing this, you need to let your readers know why they should accept your statements as valid. Tell them when, where, or how you gained your experience. Consider the following examples.

> Having raced motorcycles for five years, I have seen . . .
> My experience as a Unit Clerk in the cancer ward at General Hospital taught me . . .

Remember that individual instructors still have their personal preferences about usage and style. When they stipulate a particular technique, follow their guidelines.

Your Role as Researcher

Sometimes a research project leads you into a topic for which you have little or no prior knowledge or experience. In that case your paper will depend largely on other people's research, experiences, and opinions. However, your paper should **not** be just a cutting and pasting together of this material. Such a paper is tedious to read and does not reveal what **you** have learned from your research.

What, then, is your role as the writer of a term paper?

First, you should select a topic of interest to you or if assigned a topic, you should look for an interesting approach to the topic.

Next, you should find a **limited number of representative sources** on your topic. These you should read carefully so that you understand them and can be critical about their strengths and weaknesses. From them you should **extract** definitions, statistics, facts, examples, testimonies, and opinions that you can use in your paper.

Then, as you write to explain or argue about your topic, you should **integrate** these borrowed references into **your own explanation** of the topic. Your borrowed material--quotations, paraphrases, and summaries--should support your explanation, **not** take the place of it.

You should indicate how much agreement or disagreement there is among writers on the facts of an issue.

You should **paraphrase** difficult or technical information so it is understandable for the non-specialist reading your paper.

You should show your own originality in the focus of your topic, your selection and organization of the material, your presentation and expression, and your general conclusions.

By doing these tasks well, whether or not you add any of your own background or experience, you can bring an element of freshness to an overworked topic.

Satisfying a Need to Know

Outside academic settings, research is conducted because somebody needs the information. For example, laboratory scientists are currently investigating superconductors because there is a need to discover high-speed electronic materials that conserve electric energy. Social scientists continue to conduct research because there is always a need to discover better ways to communicate, to get candidates elected, to educate people, or to deal with the prison population.

At times you may need to conduct research to satisfy your own need to know. You may need information for making the best decision about which academic major or technology to pursue. Or you may want to inform yourself on a controversial issue before casting your vote.

In any event, you will find that the topic for your research is generally more manageable and successful if it is well restricted. For example, "Using Robots in Fast Food Restaurants" would be more suitable for a research project than "Modern Uses of Robotics."

Summary Definition

You can understand the nature of a research paper better if you remember this definition:

The research paper is a presentation of facts which are (1) based upon reading or consulting several sources, (2) presented according to a standard method of procedure, (3) integrated into the essay with your own comments and explanations, (4) limited to a relatively narrow aspect of a subject, and (5) original in selection, evaluation, expression, and conclusion.

FINDING MATERIAL--

THE EDUCATIONAL RESOURCES CENTER

Located in Columbus Hall, the Educational Resources Center **(ERC)** can serve as the starting point of your research. As its name implies, this is much more than a "library" in the traditional sense. In addition to books, magazines, and newspapers, the ERC provides a wide range of materials and services to meet your needs while at Columbus State.

Currently the Educational Resources Center has approximately 67,000 volumes. In particular, the reference collection has been greatly enlarged to support the Associate of Arts programs. The ERC has nearly 1,500 titles in its video collection. It subscribes to over 440 periodicals, 11 local and national newspapers, 16 printed indexes, and many computerized indexes.

Access to
Computer Technology

Computers are playing an ever-increasing role in the ERC, providing computerized access to indexes, reference sources, and sometimes even full-text periodical articles. InfoTrak, for example, is an easy to use index to magazines and newspaper articles of popular interest.

CD-ROM (compact disk read-only memory) indexes include <u>AIDSLINE</u> and the <u>Cumulative Index to Nursing & Allied Health Literature</u>. Reference sources on compact disc include <u>Grolier Multi-Media Encyclopedia</u>, <u>World Factbook</u>, and <u>Oxford English Reference</u>. A combination index and full-text source is <u>Ethnic Newswatch</u>. User guides are posted at the terminals and the reference librarians are available to help you. You can use CD-ROMs at two terminals in the Reference Section.

From the two CD-ROM terminals, you can dial into the Columbus Metropolitan Library on-line catalog. You can also dial into FirstSearch from these terminals. FirstSearch is an on-line collection of approximately forty databases that you can use for your research. Some of these databases are periodical indexes and others provide full text or abstracted material you can use. ERIC, MEDLINE, and <u>Readers Guide</u> are three popular indexes available on FirstSearch. For more specialized or hard to find materials, the reference librarians can conduct computer searches by accessing many different databases.

A computerized catalog--CS/LINK--enables you to find materials in the ERC by using author, title, subject, and keyword searches, among others. Also from the Status line you can tell if the material is available or if it has already been checked out.

If the ERC does not have the magazine articles that you need, it may be possible to **FAX** them in from a group of Ohio colleges and public libraries with which Columbus State shares information. Some restrictions on length of material and use of copyrighted material may apply. For help contact the Periodicals Clerk on the Ground Floor of the ERC.

The checkout process is also computerized, using a light pen to read bar codes on all circulating material. You need a validation sticker for the current quarter on your Columbus State student ID to borrow materials.

Personal computers are available too. A networked computer lab is located on the second floor. You may use the programs on the network, your own programs, or computer software from the ERC's reserve collection. You must use your own floppy disk to be able to get into the network, whether you plan to save work or not.

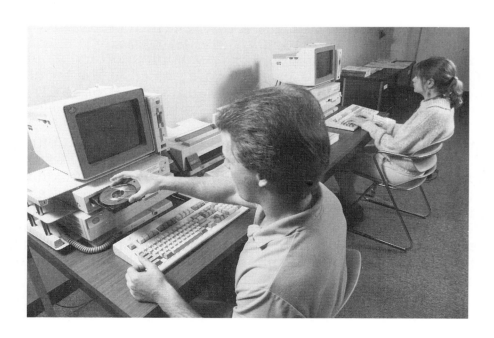

An Atmosphere for Learning

Throughout the Educational Resources Center you can see that every effort has been made to provide an atmosphere for learning. The second floor has a large collection of tele-courses and tele-modules for self-paced television instruction.

If you would like to view these materials by yourself, you should use the individual monitors in the carrels on the second floor. If you would like to view them in a group of two or more, you may use the separate rooms that have been designated for group viewing. If you need a place to work on a group project for class, you may reserve the seminar room located on the ground floor.

Regularly the Educational Resources Center hosts art exhibitions. These help to provide an attractive, comfortable place to study and work.

This overview cannot replace a full introduction to the ERC. It can only highlight some of its newest features. To get the full picture of what is there and how to use it, you should either tour the ERC as a member of a class you are taking or attend one of the many orientation sessions given every quarter.

A SEARCH STRATEGY

As a researcher in Columbus, you can find almost any kind of material that you can imagine. Often Columbus State's ERC will satisfy your research needs. If not, it is possible to use the materials of the Columbus Metropolitan Library, the State Library of Ohio, the community libraries surrounding Columbus, the local university and college libraries, corporate and industrial libraries, and inter-library loans. A list of specialized libraries is available on pages 28-29 of this book. While you may not always be able to check out materials from all libraries, generally you can get access to them and photocopy shorter items.

Regardless of which library you use, you need a logical plan of attack--**a search strategy**. Otherwise, you may waste time, fail to find needed material, and ultimately become too frustrated to complete the project.

The search strategy outlined here provides a consistent, logical plan to follow so that your library time is efficient and productive. It refers specifically to the materials at the ERC, but it is easily adapted to other libraries.

STEP ONE: Know your **TERMS.** Unless you use the correct term, you may fail to find desired material even if the library has plenty on your subject. You can locate current headings in the following sources:

Library of Congress Subject Headings
Cross Reference Index
Periodical Indexes ("**See**" and "**See also**")

STEP TWO: Spell and define your terms correctly.
Generally, you should prefer **UNABRIDGED DICTIONARIES** such as the following for your research:

Random House Dictionary of the English
Language
Webster's Third New International Dictionary

In addition, use **SPECIALIZED DICTIONARIES** in your major field if they are available.

STEP THREE: Check the **ENCYCLOPEDIAS**. No instructor wants you simply to copy a report from an encyclopedia. But besides providing excellent background and historical data, encyclopedias help in several ways.

    A.   They are **authoritative**. The writers are the world's top researchers, writers, scholars, and teachers.

    B.   They often have **bibliographical citations** directing you to other sources.

    C.   They are **concise**. By reading a short article, you can see if you have enough interest or ability to pursue the topic.

Use both **general** and **specialized encyclopedias**. The ERC carries all major adult encyclopedias such as <u>Encyclopaedia Britannica</u> and <u>Encyclopedia Americana</u>. Be aware that the focus of each general encyclopedia is slightly different, so you may need to consult several. You may check out older editions of encyclopedias located in the Main Stacks on the second floor.

Generally speaking, if there is a specialized encyclopedia for a technology offered at Columbus State, the ERC carries it.

If you are new to a technology or an academic major, you may want specific information on such topics as educational requirements, work duties, career paths, and job opportunities. The following sources can be especially valuable in getting this information:

<u>Encyclopedia of Careers</u>
<u>Encyclopedia of Associations</u>
<u>Occupational Outlook Handbook</u>

Whether you use a general or a specialized encyclopedia, go first to the **index**. There you will find all references to material on your subject.

STEP FOUR: Consult the **ONLINE CS/LINK CATALOG** for all books, pamphlets, and audio visual materials in the ERC. Public access terminals are located on all three floors, with terminals for handicapped access on the ground floor. With this system you can search for items by using the author's name, title, subject, or keywords.

A series of prompts and messages guides you from screen to screen. The last screen of the bibliographic record contains information such as call number and availability. Be sure to note the following special symbols used with the call number since they are important for finding the materials.

Ref. Indicates a **Reference** book, located in the northwest section of the first floor. Reference books do not circulate from the ERC.

L Indicates a **Large** item, located in the northwest section of shelves on the second floor.

Model Indicates a three-dimensional **Model**, located in the northwest section of shelves immediately following the Large collection on the second floor.

B Indicates **Autobiography** and **Biography**, located following the Models on the second floor.

F Indicates **Fiction**, located following the Biography collection on the second floor.

Film Indicates 16 mm **Film**, located in a separate collection at the Circulation Desk. To obtain a film, give the call number to the Circulation Desk attendant.

●　　●　　●　　●

Other format notations with the call number such as Filmstrip, Kit, Tape Cassette, Videocassette, etc., indicate items which are intershelved with the books in the Main Stacks, located on the second floor.

CS/LINK On-line Screen

EDUCATIONAL RESOURCES CENTER
Columbus State Community College

●●●

ERC CATALOG

Welcome to CS/LINK
member of the OhioLINK
Statewide Library Information System

You may search for library materials by any of the following:
        A > AUTHOR
        T > TITLE
        S > SUBJECT
        W > keyWORD
        C > CALL NO

        I > Library INFORMATION
        R > Reserve Lists
        B > CONNECT to another library

        V > VIEW your circulation record

        Q > QUIT
        Choose one (A, T, S, W, C, I, R, B, V, Q)

Please see library staff for assistance.

SEARCHING HINTS

To Search by AUTHOR:

    Type LAST NAME first, for example ----> Smith, John
                                 or just ----> Smith
    Then Press the ENTER key.

To Search by TITLE:

    Type as much or AS LITTLE of the title as you want
                   for example ----> Sports Medicine
                   or just   ----> Sports
                   or   ----> Australia
                   or   ----> Australia history
    Then press the ENTER key.

To search by WORD:

 Type in words from the title
   for example ----> Asthma & hay fever
          relieve wheezing and sneezing
   or just ----> Hay fever
   or   ----> Sneezing

Then press the ENTER key.

To search by CALL NUMBER:
   D > DEWEY Call Number
   L > LOCAL Call Number
   N > NEW SEARCH

 Type as much of the Call Number as you know
   for example ----> 402.175
Then press the ENTER key.

To do a NEW SEARCH:
 Type N for New and press the ENTER key.

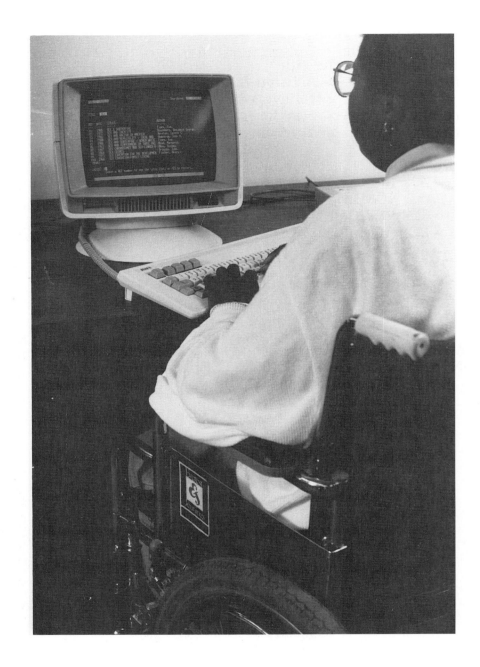

CS/LINK and OHIO/LINK

CS/LINK, the on-line computerized catalog at the ERC, is part of the OHIOLINK network which links the catalogs of Ohio's major universities, community colleges, and the State Library of Ohio. If you do not find the materials you need at the ERC in the CS/LINK catalog, you may then broaden your search at the same terminal to other labraries in the state-wide system. You can request that the materials be sent to you here on inter-library loan. Delivery should be within 48 hours of your request. Loan periods for these materials are the same as for ERC materials. Directions for searching OHIOLINK are on the computer screens. When you search on OHIOLINK, you will use the same commands as you do when you are using CS/LINK. Ask any ERC staff member for assistance at any point in your search, if you are having problems finding what you need.

In addition, several periodical indexes are included in the OHIOLINK catalog. These are listed on-screen and can be searched using the same commands as those used for searching the library catalogs. OHIOLINK is a new and growing computer network of libraries and electronic information resources. It will be constantly changing and expanding during its initial years. Changes will all be shown on the computer screens, so be aware that the system may not always be the same each time you use it.

Now consider a typical entry from the ONLINE catalog. In addition to the basic bibliographic material, it tells how long the Preface or Foreword is (the small Roman numerals), the number of pages in the book, and the height of the book in centimeters (cm). At the end of the entry you see where the book is shelved and its current status.

CS/LINK Sample

AUTHOR	Snow, David A.	
TITLE	Down on their luck: a study of homeless street people/David A. Snow and Leon Anderson.	
PUBLISHER	Berkeley: University of California Press, c1993.	
DESCRIPT'N	xiv, 391 p.: ill.; 24 cm.	
BIBLIOG.	Includes bibliographical references (p. 361-380) and index.	
SUBJECT	Homeless persons--United States	
	Homelessness--United States	
ADD NAME	Anderson, Leon, 1950-	
OTHER TITLE	A study of homeless street people.	
ISBN	0520078470.	
	0520079892 (paper)	

	LOCATION	CALL #	STATUS
1 >	MAIN STACKS	362.50973 S674d	AVAILABLE

HINTS FOR FINDING BOOKS

With the CS/LINK Catalog you can find what books, reference works, pamphlets, and audio-visual materials the ERC has on your topic. You can also use the **call number** from the catalog for finding other books on your topic.

Just follow the same general number to the different sections of the ERC.

The **reference collection** is on the main floor.

The **main stacks** are on the second floor. Also, remember that **L (Large)** books are shelved after the main collection. Be sure to check the general call number there too.

Books in the ERC are arranged according to the **Dewey Decimal System**. This system places a book into ten broad subject categories.

Dewey Decimal System

000   General Works

100   Philosophy and Psychology

200   Religion

300   Social Sciences

400   Languages

500   Science

600   Applied Science and Technology

700   Fine Arts and Recreation

800   Literature

900   History and Travel

STEP FIVE: Consult **PERIODICAL INDEXES** to find magazine and journal articles. These articles provide the most current information on events and trends, and they indicate the public reaction and attitude to incidents when they occur.

For most topics you will want to start with a general index like InfoTrac, a computerized index, since it refers to magazines and newspapers that are easy to find and easy to use. You also can use Reader's Guide, either in print or on the FirstSearch Computers. Then turn to the ERC's many additional, more technical or specialized sources until you have met your research needs.

**Examples of ERC
Periodical Indexes**

Abridged Index Medicus
Applied Science and Technology Index
Architectural Index
Biography Index
Business Periodicals Index
Columbus, Ohio Regional News Index
Cumulative Index to Nursing and Allied Health
    Literature
Essay and General Literature Index
FirstSearch (provides computerized access to
    over 40 indexes and other databases)
General Science Index
Humanities Index
Index to Dental Literature
InfoTrac **(computer)**--magazines and news-
    papers
Lodging and Restaurant Index
Magazine Index Plus (InfoTrac)
National Newspaper Index (InfoTrac)
New York Times Index
OhioLINK
Readers' Guide to Periodical Literature
Social Sciences Index

The same company publishes many of the indexes and uses a consistent format for all that it publishes. Therefore, if you can interpret the basic entry in one index, you can easily understand the other indexes.

Study this example which illustrates the basic form of an index entry.

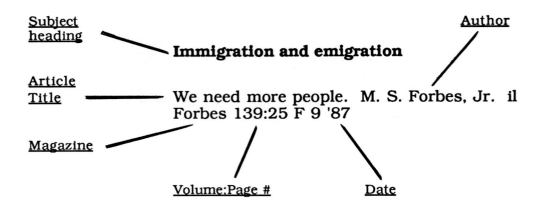

NOTE: This is **NOT** the correct bibliographical form for use in your paper. And the indexes do not always provide the first names of the authors. You will need to get that material from the periodical itself.

The correct forms are presented in this book in the section called "**The Bibliography.**"

InfoTrac

With **InfoTrac** you can conduct your own computerized periodical search. It indexes over 400 general interest magazines and newspapers. The entry also tells whether the ERC subscribes to the periodical.

After viewing the monitor to find the sources you want, push a button to print out the bibliographical data. With InfoTrac you can locate periodical articles published during the past three to seven years, depending on which terminal you use.

Here is a typical entry from InfoTrac.

RECYCLING (WASTE, ETC.)
    --analysis

        Recycling: coming of age. by Barbara Goldoftas il
    v90 Technology Review Nov-Dec '87 p28(9)
    42D3123   IN LIBRARY

NOTE: This is **NOT** the correct bibliographical form for use in your paper. See the correct form for periodicals in the section called "**The Bibliography.**"

FirstSearch

FirstSearch is an on-line computerized system that gives you access to over 40 different databases that you can use in your research. Some of the databases are general interest periodial and newspaper indexes, like <u>Reader's Guide</u> and <u>Newspaper Abstracts</u>, which serve the same purpose as InfoTrac. Others, like <u>Medline</u>, index more technical and professional-level journal articles. Still others, like <u>FactSearch</u> or <u>Disclosure</u> give you actual facts or statistics about many topics of current interest. FirstSearch is easy to use, with directions provided on the computer screen. Read the database descriptions on the screen to learn what subject and time period each database covers and how frequently each is updated.

Union List of Serials

If you need particular magazines and newspapers the ERC does not carry, check the **Union List of Serials.** Look up the name of the periodical, and this book will tell you which library in the central Ohio area (excluding The Ohio State University) carries it.

Ohio State University Libraries

To see if any of the OSU libraries has a book or periodical that you cannot otherwise find, you can call **292-3900**. The catalog assistant can help you over the phone.

Each library has its own policy on the circulation of its materials. Even if you cannot always check them out, you can generally use them there or photocopy them to take with you.

STEP SIX: NEWSPAPER INDEXES provide access to daily newspapers. The National Newspaper Index on InfoTrac and Newspaper abstracts on FirstSearch are the easiest to use and most current. Since most newspapers report important stories on the same days, you may use dates found in these indexes to find articles in your local newspaper. To find material in local newspapers and magazines, use the <u>Columbus, Ohio Regional News Index</u>. The ERC subscribes to the following periodicals indexed here: <u>Columbus Dispatch</u>, <u>Columbus Monthly</u>, <u>Business First</u>, and <u>Ohio Magazine</u>.

STEP SEVEN: STATISTICS can strengthen your presentations. The following are just a few of the sources available:

Almanacs and Fact Books

<u>U.S. Industrial Outlook</u>
<u>Information Please Almanac</u>
<u>Ohio Almanac</u>
<u>Sourcebook of Criminal Justice Statistics</u>
<u>Statistical Abstract of the United States</u>
<u>World Almanac and Books of Facts</u>
FactSearch (on FirstSearch)

STEP EIGHT: BIOGRAPHICAL SOURCES can provide information on a person's education, accomplishments, and professional activities. These sources can be useful:

<u>Contemporary Authors</u>
<u>Current Biography</u>
<u>Dictionary of American Biography</u>
<u>Dictionary of Scientific Biography</u>
<u>McGraw-Hill Encyclopedia of World Biography</u>
<u>Men and Women of Science</u>
<u>Who's Who</u>

STEP NINE: **BOOK REVIEWS** are helpful in evaluating the public reaction to or acceptance of a book and in selecting the most relevant and important titles from a bibliography.

The <u>Readers' Guide</u> indexes book reviews published in many general interest periodicals.

The following specific book review sources also are available in the ERC:

<u>Book Review Digest</u>
<u>Magill's Literary Annual</u>

Reference Librarians: At any point in your research you can benefit from consulting the reference librarians. These professionals can suggest sources for every phase of research writing from finding a topic to formatting the final draft of your term paper. In addition, some computer searches must be processed by the reference librarians. First, you should seek material from the sources outlined in the search strategy. The reference librarian can help you find and use these. Then, if you need further material or more specialized data, the reference librarians can access specialized data bases.

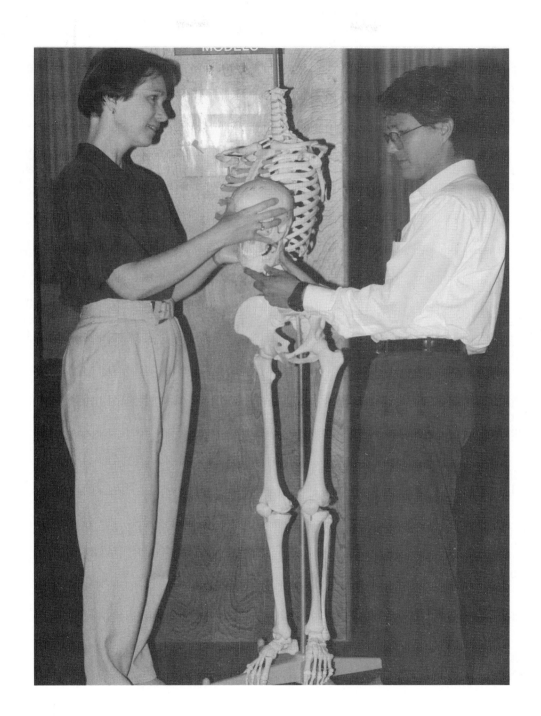

SPECIAL LIBRARIES IN FRANKLIN COUNTY

As a researcher in central Ohio, you have access to an enormous wealth of material. In addition to the school and public libraries, there are many specialized facilities. Their materials include Braille services, computer software, foreign language and genealogical materials, and government documents.

Below is a brief list of libraries that you may find helpful. Many of them do not circulate materials but allow you to use them in the library. Some libraries require an appointment. It is best to call in advance. Unless otherwise noted, the address is Columbus.

Use the **Union List of Serials** to locate periodicals in the Columbus/Franklin County area unavailable to you in the ERC. You can also search in the Ohio Technical & Community College Libraries Serial Holdings List if no local library subscribes to the periodical you are looking for. Check with the Periodicals Clerk to see if any articles you need can be faxed in from these libraries. Then, if you need further help in locating speicalized collections, work with your reference librarians. They can help you find the materials and gain access to them.

LIBRARY:	ADDRESS/PHONE:	RESTRICTIONS:
American Ceramic Society Library	757 Brooksedge Pl. Westerville, OH 890-4700	In library use
Ashland Chemical Company Library	5200 Blazer Parkwy. Dublin, OH 889-3478	In library use
AT&T Bell Labs.	6200 E. Broad St. 860-2355	In library use/ By appointment
Battelle Main Library	505 King Ave. 424-6312	In library use
Capital University Library	2199 E. Main St. 236-6351	
Chemical Abstracts Service Library	2540 Olentangy R R 447-3600 ext. 2701	By appointment
Children's Hospital	700 Children's Dr. 461-2713	In library use
Columbus Law Library Association	369 S. High. St. 10th Floor 221-4181	In library use

Franklin University Library	303 S. Grant Ave. 224-6237 ext. 252	
OCLC Library	6565 Frantz Rd. Dublin, OH 764-4340	By appointment
Ohio Dept. of Aging Resource Center	50 W. Broad St. 466-9086	
Ohio Historical Society	128 Velma Ave. 279-2510	Pass Rqd. In library use
State Library of Ohio	65 S. Front St. 644-7054	
Ohio State Univ. Libraries	1858 Neil Ave. 292-6174	OSU ID Rqd. Or courtesy card.

AVOIDING PLAGIARISM

Rather frequently, cases of plagiarism are reported in the newspapers and on the radio and television. In the 1987 presidential campaign Senator Joseph Biden was caught plagiarizing from a speech by Neil Kennoch, member of the British Labor Party. Consequently, pressure from the Democratic Party and the public forced Senator Biden to withdraw from the presidential race.

Later, a Harvard psychiatrist was caught plagiarizing and was forced to resign. His case received wide publicity across the country including a report in The New York Times.

More recently, a court ruled that Eddie Murphy and Paramount Pictures, producers of the film Coming to America, were guilty of plagiarizing a story idea submitted by columnist Art Buchwald. Mr. Buchwald was awarded substantial financial damages.

And all too often, cases involving college students arise. In fact, The Columbus Dispatch summarized a study done at Miami University which concluded that 9 out of 10 students surveyed at that university admitted to having plagiarized assignments. When plagiarism is discovered and prosecuted at colleges, the penalties are often severe, ranging from reprimand and course failure to expulsion.

What do the cases of plagiarism have in common? First, they show that the cases are widespread. But it is obvious that just because many people plagiarize, the law, colleges, and the public are not lenient when the offense is discovered. Also, cases of plagiarism set into motion a whole series of events that are time-consuming and publicly embarrassing and that can have serious repercussions.

Most important, the cases show that plagiarism can be avoided. Senator Biden could have acknowledged the ideas of Neil Kennoch. The Harvard psychologist could have used the standard academic procedures for giving credit. And Eddie Murphy and Paramount Pictures could have paid the standard royalties to Mr. Buchwald.

To avoid the embarrassment and potential dangers of plagiarism, you need a thorough understanding of what plagiarism is and how to avoid it.

Historically the word **"plagiarism"** is related to the act of kidnapping. Today, the term's use implies taking other people's facts, ideas, opinions, or organizational structures and using them as your own. It is a form of academic dishonesty which can result in several kinds of penalties. At Columbus State, you may only be required to redo an assignment. But you could receive a failing grade for the project or the course. the penalty is determined by such things as the nature of the assignment and the kind and extent of plagiarism.

Kinds of Plagiarism

Plagiarism occurs in several forms. The most obvious is the **word-for-word** use of source material without quotation marks or documentation. This is plagiarism whether the source is a book, magazine, television program, class lecture notes, or another student's paper.

A second kind of plagiarism is **paraphrasing** or restating someone's words **without giving credit** to the original. Even if you put someone else's material into your own words, you **must** give credit. And remember, paraphrasing means more than just changing a word here or there. It means restating an idea in **your own words** with **your own sentence structure.**

A third form of plagiarism is presenting someone else's **ideas** as your own. The basic facts on many topics are often fairly consistent from source to source. These may be considered **common knowledge** which needs no reference. However, the inferences and judgments based on the facts may vary widely from person to person. Also, many writers have unique ideas and opinions on topics, unique solutions to problems, and unique explanations for social and natural phenomena. You must give credit when you use their original thoughts and opinions.

A fourth (and more subtle) form of plagiarism is the use of another person's organization--the arrangement of sections in an exposition or the logical train of development in an argument. If you structure your paper according to the order in someone else's article, book, or speech, you **must** give credit.

Causes of Plagiarism

Conscious plagiarism results from the same reasons people cheat at anything else in life: laziness, indifference, a desire to beat the system, or competition for grades at any price. Whatever the reason, it is unacceptable behavior which defeats the reasons for going to college--gaining skills for learning on your own and developing your own ideas.

Unconscious plagiarism can occur because students do not know what instructors want in a paper. Usually when instructors assign written projects, they want the work to be the result of your own investigation and critical thinking. Even when you are asked to use source material, instructors do not want to see just a string of quotations and paraphrases pasted together. They want to see how you have used it for several purposes, including (1) illustrating your topic, (2) explaining terms and concepts, (3) supporting your opinions, and (4) critiquing the opinions of others.

Plagiarism can also occur because students do not understand the difference between unacceptable and acceptable uses of another person's material.

Direct Quotations

It is acceptable to use a source word-for-word **only** if you enclose the borrowed material in quotation marks and provide a parenthetical reference as the following example shows. (**NOTE:** The complete use of **parenthetical references** will be explained later. For now, simply be aware that the reference provides a link between the material that has just been cited and the bibliographical citation for that material that appears on the **Works Cited** page at the end of the paper.)

According to Cultural Literacy, "Many young people strikingly lack the information that writers of American books and newspapers have traditionally taken for granted among their readers from all generations" (Hirsch 7).

Works Cited

Hirsch, E. D., Jr. Cultural Literacy: What Every American

Needs to Know. Boston: Houghton, 1987.

No one is interested in reading long passages of borrowed material that neither indicate your response to them nor show how one piece of borrowed material is related to the next. Instead readers want the material to be **in your own words**. They want you to **restate**, to **simplify**, and to **show the connections** between borrowed passages. Readers grow bored with many direct quotations and think they might as well be reading the original.

To avoid long strings of direct quotations, you should use summaries and paraphrases.

Summaries and Paraphrases

A **summary** is a shortened version of the original **in your own words** with a parenthetical reference to give credit.

A **paraphrase** is a restatement "phrase by phrase" **in your own words** to simplify the original (often technical) material. It **may be as long or longer than the original** since it sometimes requires more words to express complex ideas that have been written in technical language. It also requires a parenthetical reference at the end to give credit to the original.

The basic problem is that students try to use too many words and sentence structures from the original. Consider the following original passage, the unacceptable summary, and the acceptable version. (The original is given as it would appear in a journal without a page reference.)

Original

> Humor delivers messages--and allows them to be received--in ways that other forms of communication cannot. Humor's ambiguity is the key to its usefulness. It enables people to say things that, if said more directly, would make others feel hurt and defensive and would threaten relationships. When people deliver such messages jokingly or laughingly, they implicitly give others permission to either take them seriously or not--or more accurately, to do both.

Works Cited

Kahn, William A. "Toward a Sense of Organizational Humor:

Implications for Organizational Diagnosis and Change." <u>Journal</u>

<u>of Applied Behavioral Science</u> 25.1 (1986): 45-63.

Unacceptable paraphrase

> Humor sends messages--and lets them be picked up--as can no other form of communication. The ambiguity of humor is the core of its utility. It lets people make statements that, if made more directly, could hurt others' feelings, make them defensive, or jeopardize relationships. When people say things in a joking or laughing manner, they let others receive the message either humorously or seriously--or both.

Here the writer has only substituted a few words of his own for words in the source. The structures of the sentences and the organization are from the original. **The result is plagiarism**.

Acceptable

> According to William A. Kahn, humor is like no other form of communication in how it sends messages and allows them to be received. Because of its ambiguity, it allows people to say things that might otherwise hurt people's feelings, make them defensive, or destroy the possibility of a working relationship. When a message is presented jokingly, the listener can interpret it humorously, seriously, or a bit of both (50).

This writer has captured the meaning of the original message, but in sentences that have original structure and diction. There are a few major words taken from the original: **humor** and **ambiguity**. This is acceptable if there are no synonyms for basic terms and phrases. In addition, the researcher has given credit for the source in a **lead-in device** and a parenthetical notation. These documentation techniques are discussed later.

Tips for Writing a Paraphrase

1. Capture the main idea of the source, but do not add your own thoughts. Save them for your comments.
2. Follow the same order of ideas as the original.
3. Use your own words and sentence structure to restate the passage. If synonyms are awkward or not available, quote the word or phrase.
4. Check your sentence for grammar and mechanics. Be sure it expresses the thought of the original.
5. Be reassured that a paraphrase can be as long or longer than the original.
6. Be sure to give credit: Use a **LEAD-IN** and a **PARENTHETICAL REFERENCE -- (   )**.

Summaries

Paraphrases are useful to help you explain a highly technical or complex idea. Often, however, you do not require the complete detail that a paraphrase produces. You may need just the main point(s) of a passage. In that case you may prefer to use a **summary**. Here is another original paragraph from the article on the use of humor in organizations. After it comes a summary which reduces the original passage to a much shorter restatement of the most important ideas. (Again, the original is given as it would appear in the journal without page references.)

Original

The theory offered herein is that humor is a means by which organization members increase and decrease psychological distance. Such calibrations are natural in organizational systems containing elements of ambiguity and politics, and composed of people typically ambivalent about their memberships. The various functions of humor help mediate the subsequent relationships between individuals and their organizations.

Acceptable Summary

Kahn explains that in organizations people are often unsure about their relationships with others and about their own roles. Through humor people can first, define their relationships and roles with others and later, with experience, can further adjust these relationships and roles (55).

Tips for Writing a Summary

1. Identify the main points of the passage.
2. Condense the main points. Try cutting out examples, restatements, explanations--without losing the **essence** of the material.
3. Use your own words to condense the passage. If synonyms are awkward or do not exist, quote the words.
4. Keep the summary **short.**
5. Note documentation facts for use in **LEAD-IN** and **PARENTHETICAL REFERENCE --** (   ).

Benefits of Summarizing and Paraphrasing

Good paraphrasing has many benefits in addition to avoiding plagiarism.

While writing note cards, you can save time by using summaries and paraphrases. Many students write long quotations on their note cards. Seldom can they use so much material. However, if you choose to write long passages on your note cards, remember to quote accurately from the source, so you can summarize or paraphrase later.

Using summaries and paraphrases in your paper rather than direct quotations shows your readers that you understand the material and can present it in your own words.

If you have questions about using source material or the adequacy of a summary or paraphrase, ask your instructor.

THE BIBLIOGRAPHY

At two points during the research and writing process, you must be concerned about bibliography forms. As you find sources for your project, you construct a **working bibliography**. Either following your instructor's directions or using your own choice, you might use index cards, notebook paper, or even a special feature on your word processor for recording this information. More important is the **format** of each entry.

The final bibliography may be called "Bibliography," "Literature Cited," or "Works Cited." The last is preferred if your research includes such non-print sources as films, interviews, or television programs. Use "Works Cited" when your bibliography contains only those sources actually referred to in the text of your paper. Use "Works Consulted" or "Selected Bibliography" when the list contains all sources you read or reviewed when preparing your paper.

By carefully recording all of the vital information for the working bibliography, you should have no problem completing the "Works Cited" page. In fact, this step should require only alphabetizing the sources, discarding those you did not use in your paper, and compiling the rest on a separate page.

However, the final step is this simple **only** if you understand what a bibliography is and how you write the separate entries.

Definition

A bibliography is an **alphabetical** list of source

materials that relate to one subject. Entries in a

bibliography **require a specific form**. And you must

use the correct form for all parts of the entry:

content, order, capitalization, punctuation, and

indentation.

MLA--The Modern Language Association Style

There are many acceptable systems for writing bibliographies and documenting papers. The following system is known as the **MLA style** (for Modern Language Association). It is used throughout the United States in colleges and universities, especially in areas of humanities and the arts. It is acceptable in classes at Columbus State unless your instructor stipulates otherwise. First, look at typical forms for a book and a periodical entry. Then we will analyze and discuss the entries.

BOOK

> Brodeur, Paul. <u>Currents of Death: Power Lines, Computer Terminals, and the Attempt to Cover Up Their Threat to Your Health</u>. New York: Simon, 1989.

PERIODICALS

> Brodeur, Paul. "The Hazards of Electromagnetic Fields." <u>New Yorker</u> 12 June 1989: 51-88.

> Paul, Bill. "Men Exposed to Electromagnetic Fields in Study Have Slower Motor Responses." <u>Wall Street Journal</u> 6 Dec. 1989: B 4.

Easy as 1. 2. 3.

You can easily remember the basic bibliography entry if you see it as consisting of **three** parts, each ending with a **period**. Study the content, order, capitalization, punctuation, and spacing in the following analysis of the parts.

1.   Author.

Last Name, First Name Middle Initial.

2.   Title.

Book Title.

"Article Title."

3.   Publication data.

Book: Place: Publisher, Date.

Periodical: Periodical Name Date: Page #'s.

Collecting Bibliography Sources

As you find sources on your topic, locate the appropriate model and write a correct entry on an **index card**. Using index cards will help you keep your bibliography in alphabetical order as you add to or subtract from it until you have completed the paper.

An alternative approach is to develop your bibliography with the help of a word processor. With your program you can create a separate file for the bibliography. On the file you can easily add, rearrange, or delete entries.

Study the final bibliographies in the sample papers to see how the finished product should look--**alphabetized and double-spaced.**

BIBLIOGRAPHY QUICK REFERENCE SHEET

Jones 14

Works Cited

magazine article:

Bolle, Sonja. "Tips on Promoting Literacy at the Local Level." <u>Publishers Weekly</u> 20 June 1968: 45.

newspaper article, signed and family title:

Buckley, William F., Jr. "Johnny's Got to Learn to Read." <u>Washington Post</u> 4 Sept. 1988: A-23.

magazine, no author:

"Business Fights Illiteracy." <u>Futurist</u> May/June 1988: 50.

film:

<u>Crisis Literacy in the Workplace</u>. Dir. Virginia Hayes. Public Library of Columbus and Franklin County, 1989.

encyclopedia entry, signed:

Golden, Hilda H. "Literacy." <u>International Encyclopedia of the Social Sciences</u>. 1968 ed.

encyclopedia entry, unsigned:

"Illiteracy." <u>Collier's Encyclopedia</u>. 1988 ed.

Quick Reference

**book with
only editor:**

Isenberg, Irwin, ed. <u>The Drive Against
Illiteracy</u>. New York: Wilson, 1964.

**book,
one author:**

Kozol, Jonathan. <u>Illiterate America</u>. New York:
Anchor, 1985.

**same author,
second source:**

---. <u>Prisoners of Silence: Breaking the Bonds
Bonds of Adult Illiteracy in the United
States</u>. New York: Continuum, 1980.

dictionary:

"Literacy." <u>The American Heritage Dictionary</u>.
1985 ed.

almanac:

"Literacy." <u>World Book Almanac</u>. 1989 ed.

**personal
interview:**

Lunsford, Andrea. Personal interview. 7 May
1990.

**journal,
continuous
pagination:**

Miller, George A. "The Challenge of Universal
Literacy." <u>Science</u> 241 (1988): 1293-99.

**newspaper
article,
unsigned:**

"Mrs. George Bush Helps Open Literacy Lab in
Columbus." <u>Columbus Dispatch</u> 15 Apr.
1988: 2 B.

article,
two authors:

Plawin, Paul, and Bertha Kainen. "Educating

Our Work Force." <u>Changing Times</u> Apr.

1988: 107.

pamphlet:

Skagen, Anne, ed. <u>Workplace Literacy</u>. New

York: American Management Association,

1986.

BASIC BIBLIOGRAPHY FORMS—A CLOSER LOOK

Having seen a bibliography in context, take a closer look at the basic forms to see what they consist of, how they are arranged, and how they must be punctuated.

BOOKS

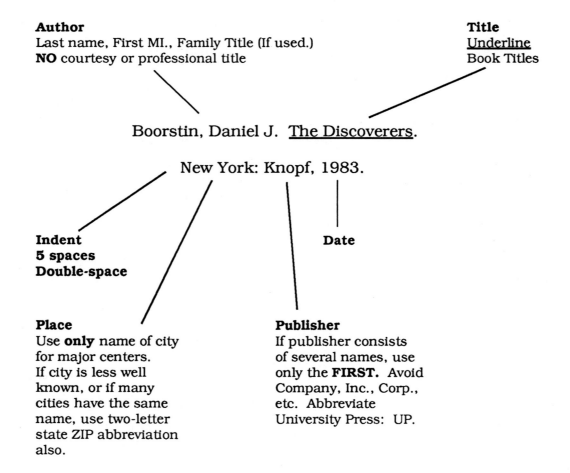

Author
Last name, First MI., Family Title (If used.)
NO courtesy or professional title

Title
Underline
Book Titles

Boorstin, Daniel J. The Discoverers.

New York: Knopf, 1983.

Indent
5 spaces
Double-space

Date

Place
Use **only** name of city for major centers.
If city is less well known, or if many cities have the same name, use two-letter state ZIP abbreviation also.

Publisher
If publisher consists of several names, use only the **FIRST.** Avoid Company, Inc., Corp., etc. Abbreviate University Press: UP.

COMMENTARY

Author

Use the fullest possible form for the author's name, as given on the title page; for example "Boorstin, Daniel J." rather than "Boorstin, D. J." unless, as indicated on the title page of the book, the author prefers some combination of initials.

Doctorow, E. L. (**NOT:** Edgar Laurence).
Fitzgerald, F. Scott. (**NOT:** Francis Scott)

If the author uses a family title like Jr. or Sr., include it in the entry thus: Buckley, William F., Jr.

Title

Provide a complete title. If a book has a main and a subtitle, use both in the bibliography. In the text of your paper, you may use just the main title. Use standard rules of capitalization for the title. Capitalize the first word, the last word, and all main words--including nouns, pronouns, verbs, adjectives and adverbs. Do use capitalize articles (**a, an, the**), prepositions, or the **to** in infinitives.

Publication Data

Use only the name of the city if it is a major center. If the city is less well known, or if there are many cities with the same name (for example, Newark, Columbus, Athens, Springfield, etc.), also use the two-letter state ZIP abbreviation.

Alaska	AK	Massachusetts	M A	Rhode Island	RI
Alabama	AL	Maryland	MD	South Carolina	SC
Arkansas	AR	Maine	ME	South Dakota	SD
Arizona	A Z	Michigan	M I	Tennessee	TN
California	CA	Minnesota	M N	Texas	TX
Colorado	CO	Missouri	MO	Utah	UT
Connecticut	CT	Mississippi	M S	Virginia	VA
District of		Montana	M T	Vermont	VT
Columbia	DC	North Carolina	NC	Washington	WA
Delaware	DE	North Dakota	ND	Wisconsin	WI
Florida	FL	Nebraska	NE	West Virginia	WV
Georgia	GA	New Hampshire	NH	Wyoming	WY
Hawaii	HI	New Jersey	NJ		
Iowa	I A	New Mexico	N M		
Idaho	ID	Nevada	NV		
Illinois	IL	New York	N Y		
Indiana	IN	Ohio	OH		
Kansas	KS	Oklahoma	OK		
Kentucky	KY	Oregon	OR		
Louisiana	LA	Pennsylvania	P A		

MAGAZINE ARTICLES

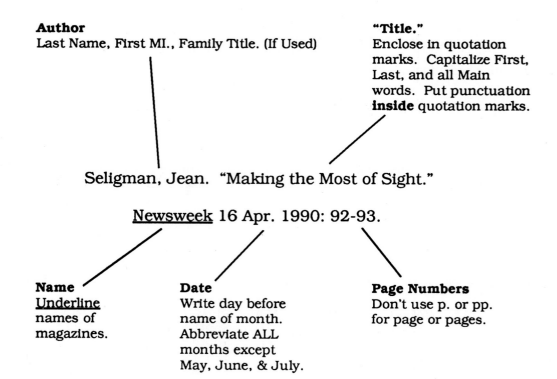

Author
Last Name, First MI., Family Title. (If Used)

"Title."
Enclose in quotation marks. Capitalize First, Last, and all Main words. Put punctuation **inside** quotation marks.

Seligman, Jean. "Making the Most of Sight."

Newsweek 16 Apr. 1990: 92-93.

Name
Underline names of magazines.

Date
Write day before name of month. Abbreviate ALL months except May, June, & July.

Page Numbers
Don't use p. or pp. for page or pages.

COMMENTARY

Author's name

Use the form as given at the start or end of the article. If no author's name is used, begin with the title. If a second or third author is present, write their name in normal order: First MI. Last.

Title

Use the complete title of the article (including any subtitle). Enclose in quotation marks: ". . . ." If a title has no final punctuation, place a period inside the final quotation mark. If a title has its own final punctuation, use it: e.g., "Onward, Women!" or "Are Animals People Too?" If the article contains any internal punctuation, use it exactly as it appears in the article:

"Education: Doing Bad and Feeling Good."
"Dissent, Dogma and Darwin's Dog."
"Metaphors of the World, Unite!"

Name of the periodical

When giving the name of a periodical, omit any introductory article ("A," "An," or "The").

NOT . . . The New York Review of Books
BUT . . . New York Review of Books

Volume number for Scholarly Journals

Use the volume number **ONLY** with **scholarly journals** not with general magazines or newspapers. Do not write the word **volume** or **vol.** before the number. Many scholarly journals use **continuous pagination**; they require just the volume number before the date, as highlighted below:

New England Journal of Medicine **321** (1989): 1577-83.

When scholarly journals start each issue with page 1, they also require an issue number:

Community College Review 16.4 (1989): 50-60.

volume.issue #

Date of publication
As illustrated above, use **ONE** space after the volume number and give the year of publication in parentheses, followed by a colon, **ONE** space, and the inclusive page numbers of the article.

For newspapers and general interest magazines, omit volume and issue numbers and give **only** the date followed by a colon, one space, and the page number(s).

28 Jan. 1990: 21-25.

Abbreviate **all** months **except May, June, and July.**

Page numbers
Cite the page number for the entire article not just for the pages you use. Write page numbers exactly as they appear on the page in the source.

If the pages of an article are not consecutive (continued later in the magazine perhaps), give the number of the first page and a plus sign (+).

NEWSPAPERS

Author
Last name, First MI., Family Title. (If Used)
No courtesy or professional title.

"Title."
Enclose in
Quotation Marks.
Capitalize First,
Last and all MAIN
words. Punctuation
comes inside
Quotation Marks.

Engleman, Robert. "Fluoride Cancer Link Unclear

Experts Say." Pittsburgh Press 27 Apr. 1990: A 9.

Publication
Underline names of
newspapers. If city
of publication
is NOT in the title,
add it in square
brackets after name,
not underlined:

Blade [Toledo, OH]

Date:
Day Month Year:

Page.
If article is on
consecutive
pages, cite
inclusive
numbers;
otherwise, give
first number and
+.

Indicate section
with style found
in newspaper:
8 F
G 13
A-22
35

Edition.
If a company prints
different editions of
the same newspaper,
indicate the edition
preceded by a comma
and a space after the date: Wall Street Journal 12 July 1992, eastern ed.: 21.

COMMENTARY

Author
Use the principles discussed for books and periodicals.

Titles
Enclose the titles of newspaper articles in quotation marks. If the title contains a short quotation or another title, use single quotation marks around it.

If the title ends with any mark of punctuation other than a period (for example, an exclamation mark or a question mark), use it. Otherwise use a period. Place all final punctuation marks **inside** the final quotation mark.

Publication Data
Omit any articles (**A, An, The**) from the name of the newspaper. Underline the name of the newspaper. If the name of the newspaper contains the name of the city where it is published (e.g., Boston Globe), you do not need to include the city. For nationally published newspapers (such as USA Today, Wall Street Journal, Chronicle of Higher Education), you may omit the city of publication. Otherwise, include the city and state of publication in square brackets after the name of the newspaper: **Plain Dealer [Cleveland, OH]**. The main principle: give your readers enough material to locate the article without confusion.

Date and Edition
Provide the date in the order of Day Month Year: **28 Jan. 1990**. Abbreviate all months except May, June, and July. Because different editions of the same paper contain different material, specify the edition (if one is given on the masthead), preceded by a comma and a space, after the date:

Columbus Dispatch 28 Jan. 1990, home final ed.: 2 B.

Page numbers
Some newspapers number pages consecutively from start to end. Some divide the paper into sections and start each section with number one. And some newspapers vary their techniques according to the day of the week. For simplicity's sake, use the style you find on the page.

BIBLIOGRAPHY FORMS--BOOKS

Author, one

Tuchman, Barbara W. <u>The March of Folly: From Troy to Vietnam</u>. New

York: Knopf, 1984.

Author, anonymous

<u>Dictionary of Franchising Organizations</u>. 1982 ed. New York: Pilot,

1982.

Author, more than one work by the same author

Sagan, Carl. <u>Boca's Brain: Reflections on the Romance of Science</u>.

New York: Ballentine, 1980.

---. <u>Cosmos</u>. New York: Ballentine, 1985.

Sagan, Carl, and Ann Druyan. <u>Comet</u>. New York: Random, 1985.

NOTE: Use the hyphen form **only** when the author unit is **exactly**
as in the preceding citation. If you add or subtract an author or editor,
do not use the hyphen form.

Authors, Two

Crews, Frederick, and Sandra Schor. <u>The Borzoi Handbook for</u>

<u>Writers</u>. New York: Knopf, 1985.

Carter, Jimmy, and Rosalynn Carter. <u>Everything to Gain: Making the</u>

<u>Most of the Rest of Your Life</u>. New York: Random, 1987.

NOTE: Write out the full last name of the second author even if that person has the same last name, as in husband and wife teams. List the authors' names **in the same order as they appear on the book** even if they are not in alphabetical order.

The order of names on the book is determined by such things as who has the higher rank, who has contributed more to the book, or how the names sound together. For instance, the sex researchers Masters and Johnson were married to each other; they chose to put the man's name first:

Masters, William H., and Virginia E. Johnson. <u>Human Sexual</u>

<u>Response</u>. Boston: Little, 1966.

Authors, Three

McCrum, Robert, William Cran, and Robert McNeil. <u>The Story of</u>

<u>English</u>. New York: Norton, 1987.

Authors, Four or More

Ehninger, Douglas, et al. <u>Principles and Types of Speech</u>

<u>Communication</u>. 10th ed. Glenview, IL: Scott, 1986.

NOTE: Et al. is an abbreviation for the Latin expression **et alii** which means "and others."

Author, corporation or institution

Worldwatch Institute. <u>State of the World, 1987</u>. New York: Norton,

1987.

NOTE: See also Government Publications.

Author <u>and</u> Editor

Plath, Sylvia. <u>The Collected Poems</u>. Ed. Ted Hughes. New York:

Harper, 1981.

Author using Pen Name

LeCarre, John [David Cornwell]. <u>The Russia House</u>. New York: Knopf,

1989.

NOTE: The author's real name is enclosed in square brackets [. . .], **NOT** parentheses (. . .). If your typewriter does not have square brackets, you should draw them neatly with a black pen.

**Alphabetized Works, Encyclopedias, and
Biographical Dictionaries**

Signed Entries

Noble, Joseph V. "The Arts--Forgery." <u>Encyclopaedia Britannica:

<u>Macropaedia</u>. 1989 ed.

Unsigned Entries

"Air Pocket." <u>Encyclopedia Americana</u>. 1987 ed.

"Wexner, Leslie H." <u>Who's Who in America</u>. 1984-1985 ed.

NOTE: Familiar encyclopedias, as shown above, need only the edition date. However, less familiar works or those under a single authorship should use a full citation, as in the following examples.

Asimov, Isaac. "Kettering, Charles Franklin." <u>Asimov's Biographical</u>

<u>Encyclopedia of Science and Technology</u>. Garden City, NY:

Doubleday, 1982.

Koegler, Horst. <u>The Concise Oxford Dictionary of Ballet</u>. New York:

Oxford UP, 1982.

NOTE: See also **Dictionary** below.

Anthology/collections of stories, poems, plays, essays or novels by different authors

Hampl, Patricia, ed. <u>The Houghton Mifflin Anthology of Short Fiction</u>.

Boston: Houghton, 1989.

Walker, Alice. "To Hell with Dying." <u>The Houghton Mifflin Anthology</u>

<u>of Short Fiction</u>. Ed. Patricia Hampl. Boston: Houghton, 1989.

1244-48.

Crane, Stephen. <u>The Red Badge of Courage</u>. <u>Eight Classic American</u>

<u>Novels</u>. Ed. David Madden. Chicago: Harcourt, 1990. 884-962.

NOTE: Use the first form when you are referring to the entire book. Use the second form when you are using just one selection, chapter, or article. Use the third form for novels or plays, that if published separately would be underlined. Notice that you must include the inclusive page numbers when using just one selection from the collection. **See also: Chapter in a Book by One Author** or **Component Part of an Anthology or Collection.**

The Bible

The Bible.

NOTE: This entry alone denotes the King James version. If you use any other version, indicate the version thus:

The Bible. Revised Standard Version.

Classical Works

Homer. The Odyssey. Trans. Robert Fitzgerald. New York: Doubleday, 1963.

Chapter in a Book by One Author

Jultz, Sam. "Emotional Health." Men's Bodies, Men's Selves. New York: Dell, 1979. 179-212.

NOTE: You must cite the inclusive page numbers when using just one chapter from the book.

Component Part of an Anthology or Collection

Henig, Robin M. "Exposing the Myth of Senility." Readings in Aging and Death. Ed. Steven H. Haret. New York: Harper, 1982. 70-74.

NOTE: If you use several articles or selections in an anthology, you should begin with the author or editor and give a citation for the entire book. In that case, do not include references to the page numbers in your bibliography entry. See also books with **Editors**.

Dictionary

The Law Dictionary. 3rd ed. Cincinnati: Anderson, 1978.

Random House Dictionary of the English Language. New York: Random,

1966.

White, D. Robert. White's Law Dictionary. New York: Warner, 1985.

> **NOTE:** Standard dictionaries can begin with just the name of the dictionary. However, when citing less familiar reference books, especially those that have appeared in only one edition or are under one author or editor's name, give the full publication data.

Dissertation

Seiter, Shirley A. "The Relationship Between Leader Behavior and the

Work Environment." Diss. Ohio State U, 1984.

> **NOTE:** Each university maintains a collection of theses and dissertations completed at that university. If the university is nearby, you can find a work by consulting the university's card catalog or online catalog. To locate studies completed farther away, consult Dissertation Abstracts International (DAI).
>
> Dissertations are often available through inter-library loan. Ask your reference librarian for assistance.

Edition

Bolles, Richard N. What Color Is Your Parachute? 18th ed. Berkeley,

CA: Ten Speed, 1990.

Editor

Gudykunst, William B., ed. <u>Intercultural Communication Theory:</u>

<u>Current Perspectives</u>. Beverly Hills: Sage, 1983.

Encyclopedia -- See Also Alphabetized Works

Signed Entries

Tietze, Christopher. "Fertility Control." <u>International Encylopedia of</u>

<u>the Social Sciences</u>. 1968 ed.

Unsigned Entries

"Rabies." <u>Encyclopaedia Britannica: Macropaedia</u>. 1987 ed.

Electronic Encyclopedia on CD-Rom

"Vegetarianism." <u>Electronic Encyclopedia</u>. Danbury, CT: Grolier,

1988.

NOTE: See the various spellings of encyclopedia.
<u>Encyclopaedia Britannica</u> retains the British spelling.

Foreign Language Titles

Hein, Christoph. <u>Drachenblut</u> [Dragon Blood]. Berlin: Luchterhand,

1985.

Introduction, Preface, Foreword, or Afterword

Boorstin, Daniel J. Foreword. <u>Simpson's Contemporary Quotations</u>.

By James B. Simpson. Boston: Houghton, 1988. vii-ix.

Postman, Neil. Introduction. <u>Teaching as a Conserving Activity</u>. By

Postman. New York: Delta, 1979. 2-12.

NOTE: When citing an introduction, preface, foreword, or afterword, start with the name of its author. Then give the name of the part being cited; capitalize the word but do not underline it or enclose it in quotation marks.

If the writer of the section is different from the author of the whole work, cite the author of the work after the title by giving the full name, in normal order, preceded by the word "By."

If the writer of the piece is also the author of the complete work, use only the last name after "By."

Page numbers in prefatory material are sometimes given in small Roman numerals (i, ii, iii) or Arabic numerals (1, 2, 3). In your citation, use whichever form occurs in the original.

Play, classical

Sophocles. <u>Oedipus Rex</u>. <u>The Bedford Introduction to Drama</u>. Trans.

Dudley Fitts and Robert Fitzgerald. Ed. Lee A. Jacobus. New

York: St. Martin's, 1989. 43-65.

In one volume...

Shakespeare, William. <u>The Tempest</u>. Ed. Henry N. Hudson. New

York: Funk, 1968.

In a collection...

Shakespeare, William. <u>The Tempest</u>. <u>The Complete Works of</u>

<u>Shakespeare</u>. Eds. Hardin Graig and David Bevington. Glenview,

IL: Scott, 1973. 1247-70.

> **NOTE:** When using just one selection from a collection, you must use the inclusive page numbers.

Play, modern

Russell, Willy. <u>Shirley Valentine and One for the Road</u>. London:

Methuen, 1988.

Poem, classical

Dante. <u>The Divine Comedy</u>. Trans. John Ciardi. New York: Norton,

1977.

Ciardi, John, trans. <u>The Purgatorio</u>. By Dante. New York: New

American, 1961.

NOTE: Use the second form only if you are referring to the translator's prefatory matter or notes to the text, not to the text itself.

Poem, modern collection

Use this form if you cite one poem in a book by one author:

Lynch, Thomas. "Like My Father Waking Early." <u>Skating With Heather</u>

<u>Grace</u>. New York: Knopf, 1986. 14-15.

Use this form if you cite one poem in a book containing works by several authors:

Rich, Adrienne. "Aunt Jennifer's Tigers." <u>The Riverside Anthology of Literature</u>. Ed. Douglas Hunt. Boston: Houghton, 1988. 1155.

Use this form if you cite a book-length poem:

Eliot, T. S. <u>Old Possum's Book of Practical Cats</u>. New York: Harcourt, 1967.

Use this form if you cite several different poems in a collection by one poet:

Kumin, Maxine. <u>The Long Approach</u>. New York: Atheneum, 1990.

Republished book

Adler, Mortimer J. <u>How to Read a Book</u>. 1940. New York: Simon, 1967.

Series, numbered and unnumbered

Ford, Boris. <u>From James to Eliot</u>. The New Pelican Guide to English Literature 7. Middlesex, England: Penguin, 1983.

Sourcebooks and Casebooks

Kreisworth, Martin. "Plots and Counterplots." <u>New Essays on</u> Light in August. Ed. Michael Millgate. Cambridge: Cambridge UP, 1987. 55-80.

NOTE: The title of this book contains the title of the William Faulkner book that the essays are about (<u>Light in August</u>). Do not underline the title of the book **within** another book title.

Rankin, Daniel S. "Influences Upon the Novel." <u>The Awakening</u>. By

    Kate Chopin. Ed. Margaret Culley. New York: Norton, 1976.

    163-165.

Translation

Suskind, Patrick. <u>Perfume: The Story of A Murderer</u>. Trans. John E.

    Woods. New York: Knopf, 1986.

Unpublished Manuscript

Finley, Charles E. <u>Introduction to Printing</u>. 1982.

Volumes, one of several volumes

McMichael, George, ed. <u>Anthology of American Literature</u>. 2 vols.

    2nd ed. New York: Macmillan, 1980.

    NOTE: In your bibliography entry indicate the number of volumes in the set. The notes within your paper (parenthetical references) will indicate which particular volume you are citing.

Added Book Forms...

Are there other book forms that are essential for your work? Record them here for future reference.

BIBLIOGRAPHY FORMS--PERIODICALS

Address or speech, published

Bush, George. "State of The Union, 1990." 31 Jan. 1990. Rpt. in <u>Vital Speeches of the Day</u> 15 Feb. 1990: 258-261.

Author, anonymous

"Re-Estimating the Risk of Radiation." <u>Newsweek</u> 1 Jan. 1990: 47.

Cartoon

Savage, Brian. Cartoon. <u>New Yorker</u> 6 July 1987: 47.

Editorial

Van Cauter, Eve, and Fred W. Turek. "Strategies for Resetting the Human Circadian Clock." Editorial. <u>New England Journal of Medicine</u> 320 (1990): 1306-07.

Zuckerman, Mortimer. "Who Stole Our Future?" Editorial. <u>U.S. News and World Report</u> 7 May 1990: 78.

NOTE: See also Newspaper Forms--Special Sections.

Facts on File World News Digest

"Oat Bran Claims Challenged." <u>Facts on File World News Digest</u> 8 Feb. 1990: 86.

Interview, published

Aquino, Corazon. "An Interview with Corazon Aquino." W. Stewart.

Time 22 Sept. 1986: 55.

Wolff, Tobias. "An Interview with Tobias Wolff." Bonnie Lyons and Bill

Oliver. Contemporary Literature 31.1 (Spring 1990): 1-16.

Journal with continuous pagination

Hoffman, Yvonne. "Surviving a Child's Suicide." American Journal of

Nursing 47 (1987): 32-39.

Reither, James A., and Douglas Vipond. "Writing As Collaboration."

College English 51 (1989): 855-867.

Journal, with each issue starting with page #1

Munter, Mary. "Using the Computer in Business Communication

Courses." Journal of Business Communication 23.1 (1986):

32-42.

Selfe, Cynthia. "Computers in English Departments." ADE Bulletin 90

(Fall 1988): 63-67.

Starkman, Jay. "Prelude to Simplification: Why Taxes Are

So Complex." Journal of Accountancy May 1990: 78-84.

NOTE: Generally, use the **issue** number after the volume number
because page numbers are often not enough to locate an
article within a volume of six or twelve issues when each
issue has separate pagination.

An alternative is the use of month or season to locate the
one particular issue as in the second model.

Some journals are like general magazines in their treatment of dates. When volume numbers are not provided, use the month and year as in the third model.

Letter to the Editor

Roth, Philip. Letter. <u>Harper's</u> Feb. 1990: 4.

NOTE: Add the label "Letter" after the name of the author. But do not underline the word or place it in quotation marks.

Magazine, monthly

Moore, Thomas J. "The Cholesterol Myth." <u>Atlantic</u> Sept. 1989:

37-60.

Magazine, weekly

Becker, Gary S. "What Our Schools Need Is a Healthy Dose of

Competition." <u>Business Week</u> 18 Dec. 1989: 28.

Review in a magazine or journal

Plagens, Peter. "The Bad and the Beautiful." Rev. of "The Golden Age

of Dutch Manuscript Painting." Pierpont Morgan Library, New

York. <u>Newsweek</u> 12 Mar. 1990: 91.

Rich, Frank. "Pain in the Sass." Rev. of <u>The Late Mrs. Dorothy Parker</u>,

by Leslie Frewin. <u>New Republic</u> 1 June 1987: 37-39.

Speech, see Address

Title containing Title or Quotation

Coddon, Karin S. "'Unreal Mockery': Unreason and the Problem of

Spectacle in <u>Macbeth</u>." <u>ELH</u> 56.3 (Fall 1989): 485-501.

Heilbrun, Carolyn G. "<u>To the Lighthouse</u>: The New Story of Mother

and Daughter." <u>ADE Bulletin</u> 87 (Fall 1987): 12-14.

NOTE: If the title of the article you are citing contains the title of a book, underline the title of the book. Contrast this with the practice for book titles containing the title of another book.

If the title of the article you are citing contains a quotation or a title of a poem, short story, or short play, use single quotation marks around the quotation or the shorter title.

Added Periodical Forms...

Are there other periodical forms that are essential for your work? Record them here for future reference.

BIBLIOGRAPHY FORMS--NEWSPAPERS

Basic Forms

Unsigned

"British Legislators OK Research on Embryos." <u>Blade</u> [Toledo, OH] 24

Apr. 1990: 1.

"Salmon Diet Good for Blood." <u>Columbus Dispatch</u> 6 May 1990: 3 C.

Signed

Newman, Frank. "Four Quick Fixes for Our Schools." <u>New York Times</u>

15 Apr. 1990: E 13.

Phillips, Jeff. "Some Speakers Are Expensive." <u>Business First</u>

[Columbus, OH] 23 Apr. 1990: 22.

NOTE: You may need special designations for some newspapers or for sections within some newspapers.

If a newspaper is not divided into sections, give the page number after the date (along with the edition, if it is stated on the front of the paper). If the newspaper is divided into sections, give the page number and section as they appear on the page.

Editorials on File

"Clean Air." <u>Washington Post</u>. 4 Mar. 1990. <u>Editorials on</u>

<u>File</u> 16-31 Mar. 1987: 334.

NOTE: If you need recent opinions on current events, this source can help. For current topics it publishes several editorials from the nation's top newspapers. Notice that the entry includes both the date of the original publication **and** the date of the republication. <u>Editorials on File</u> is published every two weeks. See how the date reflects this.

Review

Book

Johnson, Diane. "The Life She Chose." Rev. of <u>Simone De Beauvoir</u>, by

Deirdre Bair. <u>New York Times Book Review</u> 15 Apr. 1990: 1+.

Performance

Zuck, Barbara. "It's Hard to Take Eyes Off Baryshnikov." Rev. of

Mikhail Baryshnikov's Performance with Ballet Met on 23 July

1987. <u>Columbus Dispatch</u> 24 July 1987: 8 F.

Special Sections -- Cartoons, Editorials, Letters to the Editor

"Death-Penalty Politics." Editorial. <u>Christian Science Monitor</u> [Boston]

19 Mar. 1990: 20.

Guisewite, Cathy. "Cathy." Cartoon. <u>Plain Dealer</u>[Cleveland] 10 July

1987: B-23.

Thiery, Denise. "A Wanted Pregnancy Can Turn Disastrous." Letter to

the Editor. <u>Cincinnati Enquirer</u> 20 Apr. 1990: A-18.

Title within a Title

Harden, Mike. "'Platoon' Reunion Raises Curtain on Reality."

<u>Columbus Dispatch</u> 24 July 1987: 1 F.

NOTE: Titles of periodical and magazine articles are enclosed within quotation marks. Occasionally these titles will refer to or name other works such as films, television programs, and dramas. Because newspaper headlines do not use underlining, all of these titles are put in quotation marks. To distinguish the main title from the title being discussed, use double quotation marks for the main title and single quotation marks for the title within.

Added Newspaper Forms...

Are there other newspaper forms that are essential for your work? Record them here for future reference.

BIBLIOGRAPHY FORMS -- GOVERNMENT DOCUMENTS

Government publications come from many sources. Therefore, they can sometimes cause special problems in writing bibliographic citations. Generally speaking, if the writer of the work is not known, cite the government agency as the author. First give the name of the branch of government. Then give the name of the agency; use an abbreviation if the context is clear.

If you cite two or more works from the same branch of government, use three hyphens for the name in each entry after the first. If you also cite more than one work by the same government agency, use an additional three hyphens in place of the agency.

Ohio. Dept. of Motor Vehicles.

United States. Cong. House.

---. ---. Senate.

---. Dept. of Health and Human Services.

Next comes the title of the publication, underlined. When citing the Congressional Record, use only the date and page number. For other sources include the number and session of Congress, the House (S or HR), and the type and number of the publication. Congressional publications include **bills** (S 55, HR82), **resolutions** (S. Res. 25, H. Res. 60), **reports** (S. Rept. 9, H. Rept. 142), and **documents** (S. Doc. 253, H. Doc. 150).

The standard publishing information comes next:

Place: Publisher, Date.

Many federal publications are published by the Government Printing Office (**GPO** in Washington, DC). For other branches of government (state, local, and the United Nations) give the publishing information that appears on the title page.

Congressional papers

Cong. Rec. 10 Mar. 1987: S 2928-29. United States. Cong. Office of Technology Assessment. Energy from Biological Processes. Washington: GPO, 1980.

United States. Cong. Senate. Military Assistance and Sales and Related Programs. 100th. Cong., 1st sess. S 3020-21.

United States. Cong. House. National Appliance Energy Conservation Act of 1984. 100th Cong., 1st sess. H. Res. 87. Washington: GPO, 1987.

Statistical Abstract of the United States. Washington: GPO, 1990.

Executive branch documents

United States. President. "America's Economic Bill of Rights." Weekly Compilation of Presidential Documents. Washington: GPO, 6 July 1987. 764-83.

Legal citations

U.S. Const. Art. II, sec. 1.

Ohio. Const. Art. II, sec. 4.

15 U.S. Code. Sec. 78h (1964).

8 U.S.C.A. Sec. 1101. 1987.

NOTE: The United States Code Annotated contains the federal laws. Before laws are incorporated into this code, they appear in the <u>U.S. Code Congressional and Administrative Notes</u> shown below.

Water Quality Act of 1987. <u>U. S. Code Congressional and Administrative News</u>. Public Law 100-4. H. R. 1. 1987.

Ohio. Revised Code Annotated. Title XLI 4101. 1987.

Columbus Bar Ass. v. Gross (1982) 2 Ohio St. 3d 5.

Pamphlets

Citizens' Energy Project. <u>Lifestyles Index</u>. Washington: Center for Science in the Public Interest, 1977.

Miike, Lawrence. <u>Do Insects Transmit AIDS</u>? U. S. Office of Technology Assessment. Washington: GPO, 1987.

OR

United States. Office of Technology Assessment. <u>Do Insects Transmit AIDS</u>? By Lawrence Miike. Washington: GPO, 1987.

Added Government Forms...

Are there other government forms that are essential for your work? Record them here for future reference.

BIBLIOGRAPHY FORMS -- OTHER SOURCES

Art Work

Actual works

Lichtenstein, Roy. <u>Brushstrokes in Flight</u>. Port Columbus

International Airport. Columbus, OH.

Pierce, Elijah. <u>Father Time</u>. Columbus Museum of Art. Columbus, OH.

Reproductions in Books

Chagall, Marc. <u>I and My Village</u>. Museum of Modern Art, New York.

Illus. in <u>Encounter With Art</u>. Reide Hastie and Christian

Schmidt. New York: McGraw-Hill, 1964. 307.

Bulletin

Gorlin, Harriet. <u>Personnel Practices III: Employee Services, Work

Rules</u>. Information Bulletin No. 95. New York: Conference

Board, 1981.

Internal Revenue Services. <u>Statistics of Income Bulletin</u>. Publication

1136. Washington: Department of the Treasury, 1984.

Computer Abstracts and Data Base Sources

Cicci, Regina. "Dyslexia: Especially for Parents." <u>Annals of Dyslexia</u> 37

(1987): 203-11.

Computer Abstract from <u>Newspaper Index</u>. <u>Washington Post</u> 11 Nov.

1987: A-6.

Pollar, C.A., and L. M. Lewis. "Managing Panic Attacks in Emergency

Patients." <u>Journal of Emergency Medicine</u> 7.5 (1989): 547-42.

Medline 1/90-6/90.

NOTE: Use these forms if the abstract provides enough material for your research needs. Otherwise, use the abstract to find the complete source.

Be aware that some data bases do not supply complete author and title. Going to the original source can provide them.

When no author or title is provided, **begin** your entry with the words **Computer Abstract** to explain to a reader why elements may be lacking. If author and title are provided, use them. Then give the name of the data base and the inclusive dates covered by the disk at the end of the citation.

Remember to get the name of the **data base** if the reference librarian does a computer search for you. You need it for your bibliography entry.

Keller, J. C., and E. J. Kaminski. "Toxic Effects of Cu Implants on

Liver." <u>Fundamental and Applied Toxicology</u> 4 (1984): 778-83.

DIALOG Information Sources, 1985, record no. 85034898.

NOTE: **DIALOG** can help locate hard-to-find material. With the computer the librarians can locate bibliographical citations, abstracts, or the entire article if the hard copy is not otherwise available in the Central Ohio area.

"Genetech Inc." Disclosure Company, 1987. No. G122600000.

NOTE: **Disclosure** provides information about companies from data bases only, not from published sources such as books or periodicals. That is, **Disclosure** provides you with the data, not with a reference to a hard-copy source.

Computer Software

Irby, Thomas C. <u>The Graphic Gradebook</u>. Computer software and

user's manual. Swift, 1985. IBM PC-DOS 2.0, 256KB, disk.

<u>Neurological Nursing</u>. Computer software. Medi-Sim, Inc., 1985. IBM

PC-DOS 2.0, 128KB, disk.

<u>WordPerfect</u>. Ver. 4.2. Computer software. WordPerfect Corp., 1987.

IBM PC-DOS 3.0, 640KB, disk.

NOTE: There are no standardized forms for citing commercial computer programs. In general, you should provide the following if known: author; title, underlined; the identification "Computer software," neither underlined nor quoted; and the distributor or manufacturer.

At the end of the entry, add relevant information such as the type of computer for which the program is designed, the number of kilobytes and the operating system. These items are separated by commas.

Film

<u>Driving Miss Daisy</u>. Dir. Bruce Beresford. With Jessica Tandy, Morgan

Freeman, and Dan Aykroyd. Warner, 1990.

NOTE: If you want to highlight the contribution of a particular person (screenwriter, director, actor, special effects director), you may begin with that person's name and then identify the contribution.

Day-Lewis, Daniel, actor. <u>My Left Foot</u>. Dir. Jim Sheridan. With

Brenda Fricker. Miramax, 1990.

Interview, unpublished

Glenn, John. Personal interview. 15 May 1990.

Oates, Joyce Carol. Telephone interview. 15 Sept. 1989.

Letter, personal

Bush, Barbara. Letter to the author. 14 Aug. 1990.

Newsletter or In-House Publication

"Ohio House to Consider Mandatory Testing." <u>Columbus AIDS Task

Force Newsletter</u> Apr. 1987: 1.

Musical composition

Bizet, Georges. <u>Carmen</u>.

NOTE: If it's available, the complete publication data can be provided as below.

Herman, Jerry. <u>La Cage aux Folles</u>. Winona, MN: Hal Leonard, 1983.

Pamphlet

American Heart Association. <u>Nutrition Counseling for Cardiovascular

Health</u>. Dallas, TX: American Heart Association, 1986.

Scientific Affairs Committee. <u>Guidelines for AIDS Risk Reduction</u>. San

Francisco: San Francisco AIDS Foundation, 1984: n.p.

Stegner, Wallace. <u>Teaching the Short Story</u>. Davis, CA: U California,

1965.

NOTE: Treat pamphlets as you would books.

Sometimes pamphlets lack information such as dates or page numbers. Indicate this lack with **n.d. (no date)** or **n.p. (no page)**.

Product Information

The Cut, The Feel, The Lasting Quality: J. A. Henckels Cutlery.

Hawthorne, NY: J. A. Henckels, n.d.

Operating Instructions: Easa-Phone Model No. KX-T1421. Secaucus,

NJ: Panasonic, n.d.

NOTE: **n. d. = no date**

Public Address or Lecture (Unpublished)

Cuomo, Mario. "A Brief on the Freedom of the Press." Address.

Washington Press Club. Washington, D.C. 25 Nov. 1986.

NOTE: You can adapt this form to use when referring to lecture notes that you take in class as below:

Dudas, Julie. "Sanitary Conditions in the Medical Laboratory." Class

Lecture in Medical Technology at Columbus State Community

College. Columbus, OH. 3 Jan. 1988.

Recording on record or tape

Britten, Benjamin. The Turn of the Screw. Cond. Conlin Davis.

Orchestra of the Royal Opera House, Covent Garden. London:

Philips, 1984.

Marsalis, Wynton. "My Ideal." <u>Think of One</u>. New York: Columbia, 1983.

Table, illustration, map, chart

<u>Laboratory Safety</u>. Illustration. Pittsburgh, PA: Fischer Scientific, 1980.

<u>The Metric System</u>. Chart. Skokie, IL: Sargent-Welsch Scientific, 1976.

<u>Ohio</u>. Map. New York: Rand, 1986.

"Seasonal Climates." <u>Oxford Economic Atlas of the World</u>. Map. New York: Oxford UP, 1973. 3.

Television or radio program

Haas, Karl. "The Drama of Repetition." <u>Adventures in Good Music</u>. PBS. WOSU, Columbus, OH. 23 May 1990.

"Isaac Bashevis Singer." <u>American Masters</u>. Dir. William Wyler. PBS. WOSU, Columbus, OH. 6 July 1987.

Wallace, Mike. <u>60 Minutes</u>. CBS. WBNS, Columbus, OH. 24 June 1990.

Unpublished Manuscripts/Dittos/Course Materials

Thompson, Barbara P. "Techniques for Using Writing Across the Curriculum." Duplicated Handout. 1990.

Videotape

Bronowski, Jacob. "Knowledge or Certainty." Part 11. <u>The Ascent of</u>

<u>Man</u>. Video-cassette. VHS. New York: Time/Life, 1988.

Damron, James C. <u>The Credit Bureau</u>. Lecture on Video-cassette.

VHS. Columbus, OH: Columbus State Community College, 1988.

Added Bibliographical Forms...

Are there other special bibliographical forms that are essential for your work? Record them here for future reference.

MAKING BIBLIOGRAPHY CARDS MORE USEFUL

To be "correct," your bibliography cards need certain limited information in the right form and with the correct punctuation. You should **not** record factual data and notes from the source on the bibliography card.

However, books, magazines, periodical indexes, and card and online catalogs contain other valuable information about your sources that you might want to record on your bibliography cards.

While this data does not belong in the entry that you will ultimately write on the "Works Cited" page of your paper, it can be useful to you as you write your paper or if you ever want to go back and do further research on your topic.

For example, an author's academic or professional credentials (R.N., Ph.D., M.D., Professor, Fire Chief) do not belong in the standard entry. Nor does the entry contain any information about the awards or recognitions a work has received such as a Pulitzer Prize or a place on the best-seller list. However, you may want to use this information when writing the paper to help establish the credibility of the source. This technique is often used in writing **lead-in devices** as illustrated below:

> According to Milton Friedman, Nobel
> Prize winner in economics, . . .
>
> Sandra Day O'Connor, first woman
> justice of the Supreme Court, in
> writing on the abortion issue says that . . .

Therefore, do not just ignore this information when you find it. Instead, record it on your bibliography cards where you can easily find it for later use. Doing this will **increase the usefulness** of your cards.

Several kinds of information will help make your cards more useful, for example:

call number of books and magazines
name of the library where you found the material
author's credentials (from the book or magazine)
awards, honors, recognitions the author or material has received
notes on special ways the author has treated the subject--analysis,
    history, experiments, case studies, interviews
visual aids: illustrations, pictures, graphs, maps, tables, etc.

Remember, none of this information is required on your cards. But including it can increase their value. Use your judgment to decide what information and how much you want to record. With practice you will gain a better sense of what is appropriate.

The following examples illustrate how you might want to record the data on your own cards.

SAMPLE BIBLIOGRAPHY CARD WITH ANNOTATIONS

BOOK

Call Number   **Library**

331/1   Columbus State/ERC
B691w

Bolles, Richard N. <u>What Color is Your Parachute</u>? 18th ed.

    Berkeley, CA: Ten Speed, 1990.

Comprehensive self-help text for finding a job.
    Updated annually.
Cartoons lighten tone and give positive attitude.
Includes checklists for self-analysis, lists of
    agencies seeking employees, advice on preparing a
    resume, and hints for surviving the interview.

SAMPLE BIBLIOGRAPHY CARD WITH ANNOTATIONS

BOOK

Call Number   **Library**

179.3   ERC
S617a

Singer, Peter. <u>Animal Liberation: A New Ethics For Our Treatment of</u>

    <u>Animals</u>. New York: Avon, 1975.

Author educated at Oxford. Professor of Philosophy and Director of the
Centre for Human Bioethics at Monash University, Melbourne,
Australia. Book grew out of an article done for <u>New York Review of Books</u>.

BOOK

Call Number   **Library**

179.3   ERC I35 Singer, Peter, ed. <u>In Defense of Animals</u>. New York: Blackwell, 1985.   Compilation of articles by the world's spokespeople for animal rights. Authors represent such agencies as National Antivivisection Society, Animal Rights Network, Inc., and People for the Ethical Treatment of Animals (PETA). Many have academic positions in philosophy.

BOOK

Call Number   **Library**

914   Cols. Met. Lib. L649 1990   Harvard Student Agencies, Inc. <u>Let's Go: The Budget Guide to Europe</u>.   <u>1990</u>. NY: St. Martin's, 1990. Material from reports of college student travelers Includes info for planning trip, transportation, packing, health and safety precautions. All European countries covered alphabetically with major cities, maps, sights, lodging, eating spots. Also includes info of interest to gay college travelers.

PERIODICAL

Library

Periodicals Collection   Grandview Hts.

Jeffery, David. "A Renaissance for Michelangelo." <u>National</u>

   <u>Geographic</u> Feb. 1989: 688-713.

Author: Assistant Editor for <u>National Geographic.</u>
Article: Explains techniques used for restoring and
                 cleaning Michelangelo's works in Sistine
                 Chapel.
                 Includes pictures—before and after cleaning.
                 Large fold-out for close-up detail.
                 Magnified illustrations of dirt.

PERIODICAL

Library

                                        Personal Copy

"Taking the Fuzz Out of Photos." <u>Newsweek</u> 8 Jan. 1990: 61.

Article: Explains process invented by U of
                  Rochester researchers for clearing up blurred
                  photographic images.
                  Uses in aerial and satellite.
                  Contains before and after pictures.

NEWSPAPER

Library

Personal Copy

Goodman, Ellen. "Consumers Get Plastered With Labels."

Columbus Dispatch 11 Mar. 1990: 3 C.

Author: writer for Washington Post Writers Group
     winner of Pulitzer Prize for Journalism
Article: criticizes the labeling on food products;
     refers to recent statements of Dr. Louis Sullivan,
     Sec. of Health & Human Services.
     Overall tone is sarcastic.

PERSONAL INTERVIEW

Source

Lape, Sue. Personal Interview. 27 June 1990.

Interviewee: Ph.D. in English from Ohio State
Assistant Professor in Comm. Skills
Columbus State Community College.

Subject: Discussed the composing processes of contemporary poets.
     Explored the uses of "chaos" as a technique for
     encouraging originality and rewarding creativity in the
     classroom.

ORGANIZING THE EXPOSITORY ESSAY--

THE PRELIMINARY OUTLINE

As soon as you begin to gather your sources and list them on your bibliography cards, you should start reading. First skim-read for an overview; then look for specifics. But what about taking notes?

Some beginning researchers want to make notes about everything they read. Or if they are using photocopies, they begin highlighting almost every paragraph. Every quotation sounds profound, and every statistic seems meaningful. Often these researchers take many more notes than they can use. How can you avoid this problem?

Plan Ahead

State Your Purpose: Before you start to take notes, you should define for yourself the purpose of your paper. What are you going to do with the topic? Explain? Define? Argue? Compare? Analyze? Solve a problem?

Sometimes your instructor specifies the purpose. So be sure to read the assignment carefully. **"Trace the development"** means to develop the history of something. **"Compare"** means to show how one thing is similar to **and** different from something else. **"Analyze"** means to break something into its sub-parts, explain the parts, and explain how the parts work together as a whole. **"Argue"** means to take a stand or to express an opinion or judgment and to defend it. **"Explain the impact or influence"** means to discuss a cause-effect relationship.

Often you must decide for yourself how to treat a subject. You may select one of the purposes above or combine various techniques to create your own approach.

Identify Your Audience: What kind of reader should you be writing your paper for? In general, you should be writing to **lay readers**--that is, educated adults who are not professionals in the field you are discussing.

Keeping this audience in mind is important as you decide what material you must include in your paper, what technical concepts you must explain, and what technical terms (jargon) you must define.

Exposition
Outlines
Thesis

Write a Preliminary Outline: With your audience and purpose in mind, you should list those questions you must answer in your paper to fulfill your purpose.

Then by skim-reading your material, you can see which of your questions the material helps you answer or what new questions the material raises. As you read, start deciding which of your questions you **must, can,** and **ought** to answer.

List these questions to form a preliminary outline. Doing this will help focus your topic and will give your work greater direction and unity. From these questions you can later construct an overriding statement that can be developed into the **THESIS** of your paper.

Now you are ready to do a more careful reading of your sources to find the material (statistics, case studies, quotations, examples, etc.) that will help you answer your questions. Sometimes you may need to change your outline to include questions that arise during your research. Or you may need to discard questions that you cannot answer.

The following pages describe and illustrate several organizational patterns. You should see that these parts are **interchangeable**; they can be mixed and rearranged to create a logical outline. The parts are also **expandable**; you can use the same outline for a paper of 5, 10, 15 pages or more. The length depends on how much supporting detail and discussion you include.

Notice also the important role that **definition** plays in the sample outlines. By starting with, or including, a definition, you pin down for your readers the exact topic you intend to discuss. You set the stage for any further discussion or debate.

However, more is meant than just a dictionary definition. In fact, you should avoid saying something like, "According to Webster's . . ." What you need is a full definition. This consists of a basic definition **and/or** an extended definition. A basic definition can be a **formal, etymological,** or **synonym** definition.

A definition is called **"FORMAL"** when it follows the **form** or principles set forth by Aristotle. The required form is an equation. First, you place the term to be defined into a general class; then you explain how it differs from other terms in that class.

Term to Be Defined =	General Class +	Differences
triangle	geometric shape	with three straight sides and three angles
democracy	form of govern- ment	by the people, exercised directly or through elected representatives

Naturally, in the text of the paper your definition would be written out in sentence form:

A triangle is a geometric shape with three straight sides and three angles.

An **"ETYMOLOGICAL"** definition illustrates the current meaning of a word by looking at the history or derivation of its main parts. For instance, **"acrophobia"** comes from two Greek words: **akros**, meaning extreme or high, and **phobia**, meaning fear. From a study of these roots we get today's meaning of "a fear of heights."

A **"SYNONYM"** definition provides a more commonly known or less technical word for the one being defined. For example, instead of **"myocardial infarction,"** we might substitute **heart attack**. Most people are more aware of **acetylsalicylic acid** and **acetaminophen** as **aspirin** and **tylenol.**

An **"EXTENDED DEFINITION"** provides more detail through the use of history, examples, numbers or statistics, comparison or contrast, and analysis. This definition could be as long as a whole paragraph or more. Some books use an entire chapter to define the main concept being discussed. See the following definition of "substance dependency."

"Substance dependency" is a relatively new term used by professionals in the field of addiction to describe the psychological and/or physiological dependence on alcohol or any other mood-altering substance or combination of substances. It is a primary, progressive, and chronic disease. Charles Carroll, author of <u>Drugs in Modern Society</u>, states that substance dependency among adolescents is manifested by a recurrent, overwhelming urge to repeat the experience of "getting high" or intoxicated (344). Through repetition, this process becomes an automatic response which overrides all other needs. Adolescents become trapped in a cycle of drug seeking and drug using behaviors. The relationship with the drug becomes the primary concern as progressive denial of reality occurs. Eventually, all other relationships and values deteriorate.

Drug and alcohol abuse has steadily increased among adolescents in the last 15 years. In 1989, <u>World Almanac</u> reported a survey of the graduating seniors of 130 high schools. The results showed that 92.2% of them had used alcohol, and 50.2% had used marijuana during their high school years (215). Most experts in the field of addiction agree that tobacco, alcohol, and marijuana are considered "gateway drugs" which can quickly lead from experimentation to preoccupation in susceptible individuals.

Works Cited

Carroll, Charles. R <u>Drugs in Modern Society</u>. Dubuque, IA: Brown,

1985.

"Health--Drug Abuse." <u>The World Almanac and Book of Facts</u>. 1989

ed. 213-15.

For class discussion, consider the following topics. For which would you use a **basic definition**. (Which type of basic definition might work best?) Then discuss how you might plan an **extended definition** that uses the strategy outlined above.

Topics:

narcolepsy
abuse of the elderly
art therapy
subliminal persuasion
travel barriers to the handicapped
anorexia nervosa
euthanasia
lifestyles of the Amish
physician assisted suicide
dyslexia

The Extended Definition

The basic definitions are most useful for technical terms from medicine, law, science, and technology.

Some topics do not really need a basic definition. It would be possible to write one, but for most of the topics the definition is rather obvious. Consider such topics as these:

child pornography	chemical fertilizers
bridge decay	joint custody
teen pregnancy	animal rights

Instead of writing a basic definition for such topics, use an extended definition.

TYPICAL ELEMENTS OF AN EXTENDED DEFINITION

I. A Brief History

The emphasis here is on **brief**. Generally stress the most recent events of the last 5-7 years unless you must show more distant historical roots.

A. Find a starting point or something that has focused the public attention on the topic. Consider the following types of focal points.

1. Incidents: Nuclear Disaster. . . 3-Mile Island
Hazardous Wastes . . . Love Canal

2. Publications: Auto Safety . . . <u>Unsafe at Any Speed</u>

3. Movies: Wife Abuse . . . <u>Burning Bed</u>
Randall Dale Adams . . . <u>Thin Blue Line</u>

4. Court Rulings: Abortion . . . Roe v. Wade

B. Trace the Main Steps of Development.
Use chronological order.
Use events, details, facts, etc.

C. Establish the Current Status.

II. Statistics/Numbers

Through numbers you can show the magnitude, scope, or significance of the problem.

Note how important it would be to provide statistics or numbers for the following topics:

bridge decay
teen pregnancy
adult illiteracy
earthquake damage and deaths

III. Broad Examples or Categories

By sub-dividing your topic, you can show your readers the main parts. For example, when discussing child abuse, you can establish the various kinds: psychological, physical, sexual, or deprivational. In a paper on noise pollution might establish these causes: auto traffic, air traffic, industrial or home equipment, and music.

IV. Other options:

While the above points will usually be sufficient to define your topic, you may occasionally need other kinds of information. Which of the following kinds might be useful for your topic?

Descriptions: Physical descriptions of people, places, things, or processes.

Comparisons/Contrasts: Sometimes you help your reader understand your topic by comparing it or contrasting it with something else.

Analysis: Occasionally it is necessary to dissect or break down something to explain it in terms of its parts and how those parts work together.

PROVIDING CONCRETE EXAMPLES OR CASE STUDIES

In the **Definition** section, you present the broad categories or parts of your topic.

In the **Examples** section, you present more concrete details about particulars--particular people or companies, at particular times and places that are involved with your topic.

This technique allows you to **personalize your topic** for your readers. People like to read about others like themselves. To read that two out of five nurses have drug abuse problems is one thing. But a story about a specific nurse (Carol X, RN) who overdosed 12 patients when she was high on drugs is much more effective.

Also, consider the success of magazines that stress this human factor. Reader's Digest sells over 25 million copies per month by using this formula. It works.

When selecting material for this section, look for examples that are **representative** or **typical** of the whole. Readers may reject the validity of an example if it is too far out of the norm.

How many examples do you need? Sometimes one very good example makes the point you want to make.

Or if the examples are short, you may want to use more. By using two or more, you can point out comparisons and contrasts. Let the overall length of this section guide your choice here.

Guide Your Readers

Sometimes students find a workable example and include it in their paper. But they do not do anything with it. This practice is like handing the material to the readers and saying, "Here, you make sense of this."

You should guide your readers. Tell them what they will see in the example. What point are you trying to make by including it? What particular features should your readers observe about the example? Try to establish this guiding tone in your topic sentence.

Also, you may want to close the **Example** section by restating what the reader is to remember about it, how typical it is, or what attitude the readers should have formed from it.

Consider the following example section from a paper on adolescent substance abuse. Notice how the writer has used specific case studies. See how the examples are introduced. Watch how the reader is guided through the material. The examples come from the writer's own experience. They could also have come from her research.

What causes adolescents to turn to drugs? Most sources cite such factors as peer pressure, and mixed messages from adult role models. However, the major contributing factor in the development of adolescent substance dependency appears to be related to family life. Writing in <u>Social Work</u>, Joan F. Robertson concludes that adolescents entering treatment programs exhibit developmental deficiencies and poor coping skills in their personal, family, and social relationships (42). My own observations as someone who has worked as a director of a home for runaways support such findings. For example, Erica, 15 years old, is the daughter of rigid, middle class parents who have been unable to accept her learning disability. Her parents have had her in counseling f or the past year for her "low self esteem" without success. She entered treatment after her mother found notes alluding to drug abuse. She admits to having used pot and alcohol regularly for the past three years. Erica's parents rarely drink, but her grandfather died of alcoholism. Although she is experiencing despair, she cannot connect it with her substance abuse.

Jeff is a 16 year old from a broken home and has lived with a variety of relatives over the years. He has been involved in other substance abuse since age 12. He is court ordered to treatment due to a history of petty crimes. He denies having a drug problem and resents entering treatment.

Amy, a 14 year old, has been prostituting herself to supply her cocaine habit. She has been using substances since age 11 and has a history of running from her abusive, alcoholic home. She has no desire to change, refuses to stay home, and has been unable to receive proper attention from social services.

As these examples show, drug abuse starts early. It occurs as a result of many reasons. However, most cases can be linked to a dysfunctional home life.

Work Cited

Robertson, Joan F. "A Tool for Assessing Alcohol Misuse in

Adolescence." <u>Social Work</u> Jan. 1989: 40-49.

ORGANIZATIONAL PATTERNS FOR EXPOSITORY PAPERS

The following patterns illustrate basic components and organizational structures that can be used for planning your expository essay. The models can be easily adapted to fit your subject. So add, delete, or rearrange the parts as you want to create a logical, coherent plan for your paper.

The Historical Pattern

This pattern is perhaps the most straightforward. But unless the material is very unusual and startling, or the writing is very insightful, many readers find this pattern somewhat less interesting than the others.

Readers like to see the writer "do something" with the material. If you can provide a competent analysis of the data, interesting anecdotes, insightful comparisons and contrasts, fine. These techniques add interest to your writing and help your reader understand your material.

But rather than an undistinguished presentation of facts, you might choose one of the other patterns. Then if you need to include some historical background in your paper, use it as one part (perhaps in the extended definition) rather than as the pattern for the entire paper.

1. Definition

2. Examples

3. Past

4. Present

5. Future

Example

1.   How can "science fiction" be defined?

2.   What are representative examples of this genre?

3.   What early works and writers shaped the development of this genre?

4.   Who are current sci-fi writers, and what characterizes their work?

5.   What might sci-fi fans experience in this literature by the year A.D. 2000?

The Cause-Effect Pattern

This pattern works well with many kinds of topics: explanations of products, techniques, medical or social problems, and controversies. Here are the main parts of this pattern.

1.   How is the topic defined?

2.   What are prime examples of it?

3.   What are the main causes?

4.   What are the main effects?

5.   Possible final question: solutions?
                                                         treatments?
                                                         public or professional reactions?

Example

1. What is meant by "television violence?"

2. What do specific examples show about types and explicitness?

3. What motivates programmers to include violence in their schedules?

4. What do critics cite as the undesirable effects of television violence?

5. What steps are being taken to restrict the showing of television violence?

The Problem-Solution Pattern

While this pattern presents a solution to a problem, it is **not necessarily your own solution**. Presenting and defending your own solution would change your purpose to argumentation. In exposition you are basically reporting and explaining what you believe to be the most logical or valid solution that you have discovered during you research.

1. How is the topic defined? (The Problem)

2. What are examples of the topic?

3. What solutions are being proposed?

4. Possible options: causes
opinions of witnesses or experts
secondary problems/issues

Example

1. What do statistics show about the declining numbers of teen-agers available to work in America's fast food industry?

2. How has this problem been recognized by specific local fast food chains?

3. What present measures are being taken to solve this labor problem?

4. What long-term steps are being considered?

5. Possible options: minimum wage issue
   controversies about effect of
   employment on teens' schooling

The Advantages-Disadvantages Pattern

Sometimes the other patterns just do not seem to fit a subject. At such times you might consider the Advantages-Disadvantages pattern. It works particularly well with discussions of products, techniques, and social or technological developments. Here are its main components.

1. How is the topic defined?

2. What are specific examples of the topic?

3. What are the disadvantages?

4. What are the advantages?

5. Possible options: importance of topic
   direction for future
   implications for research,
   a technology, etc.

Example

1. What are "cellular mobile phones?"

2. What are specific examples of systems available in the Franklin County area?

3. What are the disadvantages of phones in cars?

4. What are the advantages?

5. What are the laws concerning use, abuse, and insurance liability?

The Topical Pattern or
The Journalistic Pentad

You are probably familiar with the basic questions all reporters are supposed to consider in planning a story. These questions are called the journalistic **pentad** (from Greek, meaning **a group of five**). Here are the five questions and their explanations.

1.   **Where** and **When** =   the **Scene**, the location and time

2.   **Who**   =   the **Agent**, the doer, the person involved

3.   **What**   =   the **Action**, What happened?

4.   **How**   =   the **Agency**, How was it done?

5.   **Why**   =   the **Purpose**, What was the motive?

You, too, can use these questions. With them you can probe into your topic and find the points you might discuss. Later you can use them to structure your final essay.

Notice, however, that not just any five questions will do. The questions must be relevant and logical. They must work together to give a whole picture of the topic.

Example

1.   Who is Leslie H. Wexner?

2.   What is the history of the development of the Limited?

3.   How has the Limited gained such a large share of the retail clothing market?

4.   Why has Wexner played a leading role in the development of the cultural and artistic life of Columbus?

5.   Besides the arts, where else in Columbus can one see Mr. Wexner's contributions?

The Career Search Pattern

Too often students select a major without a clear understanding of the educational requirements, responsibilities to be performed, job opportunities, and salary. Some students use a research paper assignment as a chance to explore their major as a career choice.

The outline is, in essence, a topical arrangement, in that you choose the topics or questions that you believe are most important to you.

Here is a list of the typical questions. Select or develop questions that are relevant; that are important to you; and that, when combined, create a logical, coherent outline.

Career Question Bank

1. What are the educational requirements?

2. What responsibilities is a person expected to perform on the job?

3. What are the opportunities for career advancement within the field or from one field to another?

4. What is the salary range, and what factors affect the salary?

5. Where are the jobs?

6. What are the attitudes of workers in the field to their jobs?

7. What does the future hold for careers in this job?

8. Are some personality types more suited to this career than others?

9. What occupational dangers (physical, emotional, financial) does one face in this field?

10. Who are good role models to study in this field?

Other Questions:

Example

1. Who has the educational background and experience needed to be an insurance agent?

2. What are the varied job duties performed by an agent?

3. How well compensated is an agent, and what factors contribute to salary and benefits?

4. How does an independent agent compare with one employed by an insurance company?

5. Where in the country are the best job prospects for a young agent?

PHRASING MAIN POINTS IN YOUR OUTLINE

All of the outlines already illustrated have used questions. In an expository paper you are explaining a topic to someone who is otherwise unfamiliar with it. One way to approach the task is to ask yourself what the reader needs to know to understand the topic. This approach justifies the use of questions to guide your development.

Also, the above outlines are preliminary tools. They help you focus and shape your work, and they keep you on a steady course so that you do not drift while you are developing your paper. They are a check on your paper's unity.

But not all outlines need to use questions. They may use words, phrases, or full sentences. They can also show your sub-points. Follow the directions of your instructor. But be consistent! Do not mix the techniques for phrasing main points.

To illustrate alternative phrasing patterns, one question outline from above has been reworked to illustrate sentence, phrase, and formal outline forms.

Sentence Outline

1. "Television violence" is defined in a variety of ways.

2. Just one week of television programming contains many types and degrees of violence.

3. Television executives offer such programs for several reasons.

4. Critics attribute many undesirable effects to watching television violence.

5. Concerned groups have formulated plans to limit and regulate the showing of television violence.

Phrase Outline

1. "Television violence" defined.

2. Types and degrees of violence.

3. Motives for televising violence.

4. Undesirable effects of television violence.

5. Steps to limit and regulate television violence.

Formal Outline Showing Sub-Points

I.   "Television violence" is defined in a variety of ways.

II.   Just one week of television programming contains many types and degrees of violence.

      A.   Police shows contain brutal shootings.

      B.   Daytime soap operas simulate acts of domestic violence.

            1.   Rape and date rape are often depicted.
            2.   Many episodes revolve around spouse abuse.
                  a.   In a recent segment of <u>Loving</u> . . .
                  b.   An episode of <u>America's Most Wanted</u> simulated . . .

                    i.

                    ii.

III.   Television executives offer such programs for several reasons.

IV.   Critics attribute many undesirable effects to watching television violence.

V.   Concerned groups have formulated plans to limit and regulate the showing of television violence.

Writing the Expository Thesis

Your thesis statement may begin as a tentative expression of your paper's main point. You can adjust this early statement as you read more and begin assembling your own ideas and research findings into a draft. In its final form, your thesis statement must be clear and specific, for it makes a promise to your reader about what will come in the rest of the paper. Generally, your thesis should contain two elements: the exact subject of your essay and a phrase that further limits this subject. You can see how important the restricting word or phrase is from the following examples, which show how one topic may be limited in different ways.

Topic	Possible Restricting Phrases
	has grown beyond scientific research to applications in commerce, administration, education, and the arts.
	has created a new set of health-related problems which challenge office workers and employers.
The Computer Science Technology	has redefined the printing industry through the use of desk-top publishing.
	offers women unique opportunities for economic benefits and professional advancement.

As you can see, a clear thesis often suggests a method of development. In each of the above thesis statements the subject is the same. But each restricting phrase points to a different method of development. The first thesis implies a topical order, with each sub-topic an area in which Computer Science Technology has had an impact. The second thesis suggests a problem-solution order, discussing the health problems related to computer science and their possible solutions. The third thesis indicates a cause-effect order, discussing the impact of computers on publishing. The fourth thesis indicates a career-search strategy (usually a topical) order, focusing on women in Computer Science.

Thesis Statement: Some Options

Your restricting phrase will usually imply the kind of organizational pattern you have selected for your paper. For a cause-effect order you might stress the impact or effect of your topic on a technology or on some group of people.

Cause-Effect

The fast food industry has changed how Americans think about food and meal time.

The Maxxum 7000 has transformed many amateur photographers into virtual professionals.

Importance of Topic

Often when you select a topical order, no specific thesis indicates this approach. You might then choose to establish the importance of your topic.

The uncontrolled dumping of nuclear wastes has threatened the residents of many communities.

Direction of Growth or Decline

You may want your thesis to indicate the direction of growth or decline your topic is taking.

An increasing number of computer users are victims of repetitive motion syndrome.

Once overcrowded, the market for engineers is opening for the 1990s.

Complex Sentences

So far, the examples of thesis statements have been simple sentences. Sometimes you may want more than this. You may want a **dependent clause** which will link your introductory comments with the thesis, which points to the rest of your paper. At such times a **"Because . . . ,"** **"Since . . . ,"** or **"Although . . . ,"** can be helpful.

EXAMPLES:

Because more cases are being reported and prosecuted, the physical abuse of the elderly has become recognized as a significant social problem.

Since the teen-age labor pool has declined and fast food restaurants must pay premium wages to attract help, businesses are looking to technology for a new source of labor for the 1990s--robots.

Although nursing is no longer one of a few career options open to them, many intelligent women still consider it the profession of choice.

Notice that the introductory clauses **point back** to the material that would have been used in the opening of the essay. In the first example, the writer would have established the growing number of elder abuse cases that have been reported and prosecuted. The rest of the essay could be developed as a cause-effect or more likely as a problem-cause-solution.

Remember, for this technique to work, the dependent clause **must come first.** Otherwise, the direction signals get mixed, and the reader can become confused.

Thesis Statements:

The organizing sentence is called a **thesis statement**. This implies that it should be just that:

a complete declarative sentence.

When writing a thesis, you should avoid the following pitfalls.

PITFALLS TO AVOID

A thesis is

_ _ _ _ _	**Not a Fragment**	The role of robots in auto manufacturing. **This might work as a title.**
_ _ _ _ _	**Not a Question**	What is meant by an "electro-magnetic field?" **This could be a topic sentence.**
_ _ _ _ _	**Not a Command**	Let's consider the causes, effects, and treatments of teacher burnout. **This might come in the introduction after the thesis to outline the main parts of your paper for your reader.**
_ _ _ _ _	**Not a Definition**	**Bulimia** is a dietary abnormality found most often in teen-age girls and is characterized by periods of binging on large amounts of food followed by periods of purging through vomiting. **A definition does not provide any direction for further development.**
_ _ _ _ _	**Not a Statement of Fact or Statistic**	The average beer-drinker in the U.S. consumes over 365 cans of beer per year. In a Pennsylvania study, college students reported that they thought about sex approximately 300 times per day. **Statistics and facts can develop a topic sentence; they do not provide a direction for further development.**

_ _ _ _ _	**Not Source Material**	In "Baby Blues Gone Mad," Fern Chapman reports that doctors are gaining new insight into a severe form of mental illness among new mothers: postpartum depression. **Citations can help introduce your paper or can develop a topic. Let your thesis be your own generalization.**
_ _ _ _ _	**Not Obvious**	If people want a career in Animal Health, it is vital that they get along with animals. **Provide a bit more insight.**
_ _ _ _ _	**Not an Opinion/ Value Judgment**	Due to understaffing and low budgets, many nursing homes provide inferior health care. **This is argumentative; your purpose in exposition is to explain.**

ORGANIZING THE ARGUMENTATIVE ESSAY

The definition of the research paper which appears on page 5 of this guide focuses mainly on the expository paper because that is the type most often specified in college papers--especially for beginning researchers. However, many assignments require you to do more than report the current status of a topic. You are expected to be able to define a specific **issue**, research it, take a position on the issue, and defend that position. This is the process known as **argumentation**.

Philosophers, theorists, and practitioners from Aristotle onward have explored and written on argumentation. As a result, the techniques and theories of argumentation fill many massive volumes. Indeed, a thorough treatment of argumentation could occupy a whole course or an entire professional career.

It is impossible here to offer a comprehensive treatment of argumentation. Instead the following pages attempt to give you some of the basics on planning and structuring an argumentative paper. This section defines for you what an argumentative **issue** is, explains the three basic kinds of issues, and then illustrates the organizational structures you can produce with them.

TOPIC VS. ISSUE

When asked what **issue** they are doing their papers on, many students respond by naming a **topic** like divorce, AIDS, or suntan parlors. While these may be sound topics they are not yet argumentative issues.

An argument refers to a discussion in which there is disagreement--at least two sides of an issue. In argumentation, **an issue is a specific point of controversy usually phrased as a question**. Argumentative papers may center on an issue of **fact**, an issue of **value**, or an issue of **policy**. Determining the kind of issue in dispute is the first step in writing the argumentative paper, for it will affect both the content and organization of your paper.

FACT ISSUES

Be careful not to confuse **questions of fact** with **issues of fact**. A question of fact is like one of the following:

Who won the Academy Award for Best Actress in 1990?

What is the literacy rate of Bangladesh?

How does one perform the Heimlich Maneuver?

Such questions of fact can be answered absolutely. You can look up the answers in a reference book. The answer is right or wrong. But there is no argument.

Issues of fact cannot be answered so absolutely. There **is** a right answer, but we do not have sufficient information to know it. Issue questions fall into four general types.

QUESTIONS OF REALITY OR EXISTENCE

Is "X" real? or **Does "X" exist?**

Is there intelligent life on other planets?
Is PMS a real disease?
Does racial discrimination exist in the city's police department?
Is this painting really by Picasso?
Do UFOs exist?

QUESTIONS OF CAUSALITY: CAUSE-EFFECT

Does "X" cause "Y"?

Does caffeine improve the sex lives of senior citizens?
Does television violence promote aggressive tendencies in children?
Does working at a video display terminal (VDT) harm a person's health?
Does oat bran reduce blood serum cholesterol?

QUESTIONS OF PREDICTION

Will "X" happen?

Will the President be elected for a second term?
Can scientists halt the destruction of the ozone layer by the year
2000?

INTERPRETATION OF EVIDENCE

Can "X" be interpreted to show "Y"?

Did Lee Harvey Oswald act alone in the assassination of President
Kennedy?
Are the Egyptian pyramids the work of extra-terrestrials?
Was Cleveland resident John Demjanjuk the Nazi camp guard known
as "Ivan the Terrible?"

No one has the final answers to these questions, but that does not stop
people from speculating about them or from trying to convince others that
they have the best available answers.

While final answers are not known, certain facts, opinions, statistics,
and testimonies exist for all of these topics. In dealing with a fact issue, you
gather data and determine which of it is relevant for establishing and
defending an opinion. For instance, on the issue of racial discrimination in a
police department you can establish the following facts:

The employment statistics for a specific period:
Who was hired?
What percentage was men? Women?
What percentage was Caucasian, Black, Hispanic, and Asian?

After a specified period:
What percentage of the original remains?
What reasons were cited for those who left?
What percentage of each group remains?
What percentage of each group was promoted?

What specific programs were used to recruit officers?
Did recruiters work as hard for minorities as for whites?

Similarly, for other fact issues you need to discover what criteria must be fulfilled to take a defensible position and what data is available and relevant for meeting the criteria.

Argumentative papers on questions of fact are usually organized **topically**. Suppose, for example, you want to convince your readers that the president's economic policy will prevent an economic recovery. Each main point will present a **reason** why your readers should agree with you.

Thesis: The President's economic policy will prevent an economic recovery.

1. The policy of deficit spending has continued unchecked.

2. Increased taxes will discourage foreign investors.

3. Little has been done to refurbish America's heavy manufacturing.

4. New environmental safeguards may stifle the logging and petroleum industries.

Occasionally you could arrange an argument of fact **spatially**. For example:

Thesis: UFOs are real phenomena as reported by eyewitnesses throughout the country.

1. On the east coast, Maine fishermen have . . .

2. In the Appalachian Mountains, hikers saw . . .

3. Farmers on the Great Plain have reported . . .

4. Astronomers in California . . .

Notice that in these examples, the writer's purpose is limited to persuading the readers to accept a particular view of the facts. Sometimes, however, a controversy generates an argument that must go beyond an issue of fact and will turn into an issue of value.

VALUE ISSUES

Who was the best American president? Is it morally justifiable to use aborted fetal material to help patients with Alzheimer's disease or Parkinson's Disease? How safe is our drinking water? While answering such questions requires factual evidence, testimonies, and opinions, these questions also require **value judgments**--judgments based on a person's own beliefs about the worth, merit, or value of something. These statements focus on what is right or wrong, good or bad, moral or immoral, ethical or unethical, helpful or harmful. Notice that a value judgment must contain one of these or a comparable value term.

Consider the issue of the research with fetal material. You can discuss it from a purely factual basis by answering such questions as these: "How much material is available for research?" "What parts are used?" "How is it collected?" "How has the processed material been used so far?" "What have been the results?" These are questions of fact. Your answers summarize and report the information you gather; they do not reflect your own beliefs or value system regarding the practice of research using aborted fetal material.

But suppose you ask "Is it morally justifiable to use aborted fetal material in laboratory research?" Now you have raised an **issue of value**. Your answer to the question depends not only on what factual knowledge you gather but also on what moral values or system of ethics you have developed throughout your life.

Yet your answer to a question of value cannot depend only on your own opinion or value system. An argument requires evidence. You must decide what standards or criteria must be met to justify your value opinion. Suppose you claim that vegetarianism is the best lifestyle to follow. Your first step is to explain what you mean by "best" lifestyle. Is it one that is healthy? That is inexpensive? That is relatively easy to follow? That makes the optimum use of a country's natural and animal resources? By defining "best" lifestyle, you establish your criteria.

For class discussion, consider each of the following questions of value. What standards or criteria would you want to extablish before reaching a decision on the issue? What kind of specific evidence (statistics, facts, example, or testimony) might you use to support the standards?

Value Issues:

1. How acceptable is it for women to retain their maiden name after marriage?

2. Is it beneficial for parents to educate their children at home rather than sending them to public schools?

3. To what extent are multiple vitamins healthy?

4. How desirable is a career in the military?

Once you establish your criteria, you need to arrange them in a logical order. Many value arguments use a **topical order**. Often the main points are arranged from least to most important from your readers' point of view.

Consider the following outline.

Option A -- Thesis and Support

Thesis: For modern Americans, vegetarianism is the best lifestyle to follow.

1. Vegetarians receive philosophic comfort in the knowledge that no animal has been slaughtered to provide their meals.

2. Vegetarianism makes optimum use of the world's limited natural and economic resources.

3. With little effort, vegetarians receive a complete assortment of protein and other essential nutrients.

4. Vegetarians avoid the harmful chemical additives found in today's meats.

5. This diet decreases one's chance of developing certain health problems and improves the likelihood of surviving others.

Option B -- Two-Part Thesis
Acknowledging the Opposition

In argumentation, speakers and writers often use the technique known as **acknowledging the opposition**. For example, in the preceding outline you might acknowledge the fact that Americans are culturally used to the taste of meat and associate it with meals from the Thanksgiving turkey to the summertime barbecue. Or you could grant the point that many jobs in the nation's economy depend on the production and consumption of meat.

Then, you could refute the opposition by showing its weaknesses. For instance, you can refute the first point by showing that it is possible to change culturally determined tastes by educating people about the dangers of meat consumption. Or you can simply give up the opposing points. Admit that they exist, and then move on to show that the points on your side are more important. Either strategy can help to draw your reader to your side. Notice also that you should organize the points for your side in <u>climactic order</u>, from least to most important from your readers' point of view.

If you acknowledge your opposition, it is best to do it **before presenting your own case**. Also be sure to adjust your thesis to reflect this approach:

Thesis:　Although Americans are culturally conditioned to be meat eaters and benefit economically from the meat industry, vegetarianism is the best lifestyle for the 1990s.

1.　Americans are culturally conditioned to be meat eaters.

2.　The country's economy benefits from the production and consumption of meat.

3.　Vegetarians receive philosophic comfort from the knowledge that no animal has been slaughtered to provide their meals.

4.　Vegetarianism makes optimum use of the world's limited natural and economic resources.

5.　By following simple principles of protein complementary, vegetarians receive all essential nutrients.

6.　Vegetarians avoid the harmful chemical additives found in today's meats.

7.   This diet decreases one's chance of developing certain health problems and improves the likelihood of surviving others.

For class discussion, return to the list of criteria you established for the value questions above. How would you arrange them in order of importance for the readers of an essay. It is apparent that a value issue can have important implications for our actions. People who are persuaded by the argument for vegetarianism may be inclined to change their buying and eating habits. They may encourage their friends to become vegetarians. Or they may go so far as to become advocates for animal rights. However, papers on questions of value do not argue for or against any particular law or rule or for any specific course of action. They do not urge readers to **do** anything. If you go beyond arguing right or wrong to arguing that something should or should not be done, you move from a question of value to a question of policy.

POLICY ISSUES

When you approach a topic by taking a stand on **what should be done about it**, you are generally dealing with a policy issue. Policy issues generally fall into two categories:

1.   Rules, Laws, and Regulations

These are codes or standards that regulate our actions. Virtually every aspect of our life can be regulated by some rule or law. How fast we drive on the freeway, how old we must be to purchase alcohol, what architectural changes we are allowed to make to our homes--all of these activities are defined by laws and can be enforced. Note the relationship between the verb **"police,"** meaning **to enforce** and the noun **"policy."** Consider some of the policy questions debated at all levels from international to personal.

2.   Courses of Action

Courses of action can be of many kinds. Some deal with how money, land, or natural resources will be used. For example:

Should Ohio build a high-speed passenger rail system to link Cleveland, Columbus, and Cincinnati?
Should Columbus State provide child care for students, faculty, and staff?

Other courses of action call for a specific solution to a problem. For example:

> Should the mandatory seat belt law be repealed?
> How should the United States deal with teen drug abuse?
> How should the city meet its need for water?

Policy issues occur daily in almost every aspect of life from questions of international relations to questions of personal matters. Consider some recent policy issues at a range of levels.

International:

> Should the U.S. maintain trade sanctions against South Africa?
> Should the world's nations permit mining in Antarctica?

National:

> Should gays and lesbians be permitted to serve in the U.S. military?
> Should logging be regulated in the northwest to protect endangered species?

State:

> Should Ohio permit casino gambling?
> Should Ohio landfills accept medical wastes from other states?

Local:

> Should Columbus build a sports arena?
> Should Columbus adopt a mandatory recycling law?

Personal:

> Should families consider transracial adoption?
> Should parents provide a home-based education for their children?

Note: Some personal policies are really value issues in disguise. It is often better to rephrase them and treat them like value issues.

For example, the above policy questions would work just as well if turned into value questions like these:

How desirable is transracial adoption?
To what extent is it desirable for parents to provide a home-based education for their children?

Most of the above examples show how a policy can institute a new law or define a new course of action. Yet a policy issue can do any of the following:

Establish a policy	Times and conditions change. As new lifestyles and technologies emerge, new policies are needed to meet these changes.
	Should the piracy of computer programs be prosecuted?
Change a policy	Perhaps not a wholly new policy is needed, just a change in the old.
	Should the method of electing a president be changed?
Enforce a policy	The law may be already on the books. It may simply need to be enforced.
	Should the leash laws be better enforced?
Maintain a policy	You may be perfectly content with some policies and want them to be preserved.
	Should the law banning smoking from short air flights be preserved?
Abolish a policy	A law may no longer be applicable because of changing technology, lifestyles, sociology, etc.
	Although not enforced, many old laws stay on many city, state, and federal books.
	Should the city's jaywalking law be abolished?

Basic Elements of a Policy Argument

In general, you must provide three basic elements to construct a solid policy argument. These elements are **need, plan,** and **practicality.**

Unless you can establish a **need**, there is no point in arguing for a policy change.

Is there a need for a child-care facility on campus?
Is there a need to control drug sales to youth?
Is there a need to build a sports arena?

Your first step is to convince readers that there is a problem with the current situation. Without clear evidence that there is a legitimate problem, readers will be reluctant to adopt a proposal for change. You must define the problem and illustrate it with a selection of facts, examples, case studies, testimonies, and opinions. However, if you are defending the present policy, you must show that current conditions are acceptable.

The second element is **plan**. Here you outline a specific solution to the problem, outlining as many of the particulars as space and your technical understanding permit. What would the parts of the solution consist of?

What can be done to develop a child-care facility on campus?
What particular steps should be taken to control the
sale of drugs to youth?
What property sites exist? How can they be acquired?
Who will fund the project?
What national sports franchise can be acquired?

Such questions are especially critical if you want to establish a new policy. Unless they receive a specific, detailed plan, many readers will remain unconvinced that they should do anything different from what they are presently doing. It is unlikely that you will have a thorough understanding of all of the legal, social, and technological aspects of a project. Yet you should do your best to list the main components of a plan and to explain them to the best of your ability. For example, with the topic of a sports arena you could establish the following: the sites available for construction, the ability of the city or county to acquire them, the potential funding sources, and the potential sports franchises that could be acquired. To show the feasibility of the plan, you could also compare Columbus with other cities (like Indianapolis) that have built arenas.

The final element is **practicality**. Here you establish first the <u>specific</u> benefits; namely, the resolution of the problem. Then you present any <u>general</u> or fringe benefits that adopting the plan would produce. For instance, will money or time be saved? Will the environment be cleaner?

> A child-care facility can improve the lives of the children and parents. It would be a good public relations tool for the college, and could be a vital component of the college's child-care technology.

> An effective drug education program can save the lives of young people. It could break the drug abuse-crime-incarceration cycle, and it would be less costly than drug rehabilitation programs.

> A sports arena can satisfy the city's sports fans. It could also be used for concerts. It would attract visitors to the city and convention trade, and it would create many jobs.

These outcomes are important. If you present a new policy, you must be able to show that it at least addresses the problem it is designed to correct. Sometimes new policies create their own problems: money must be spent, people's lives can be disrupted, and limited resources are used up. You should show that your policy creates fewer problems than it solves. Ideally the new policy will also give you a chance to do a certain amount of crowing about its benefits.

But if your purpose is to maintain the current policy, your goal must be to show that it will be more beneficial to maintain the status quo and that any change will create more severe problems than any that currently exist.

For class discussion, consider each of the following policy questions. For each, decide what materials would be required to establish the three sections of Need, Plan, and Practicality.

1. Should companies and governmental departments located downtown adopt carpooling policies?

2. Should abortion pill RU 486 be available by perscription in the United States?

3. Should living wills be legalized in Ohio?

4. Should employees be subjected to random drug testing?

5. Should people support organ donation programs?

Organizing Policy Papers

Many students find that their policy arguments fall easily into a **problem-solution order**.

INTRODUCTION

I.   Gain attention and establish good will

II.   Develop credibility through use of source material.

III. Establish specific policy issue.

IV.   Present thesis.

BODY

I.   Explain problem.
      A.   Describe symptoms or results of problem.
      B.   Illustrate its size and/or significance.
      C.   Discuss its cause(s).

II.   Present solution.
      A.   Explain solution.
      B.   Show how solution eliminates problem.
      C.   Outline added benefits to be gained.

CONCLUSION

I.   Appeal for policy recommendation to be accepted.

II.   If audience needs to respond, explain action to be taken.

III. If no action is needed, you might close with the promise of a better tomorrow, or a warning about what might happen if the policy is not adopted.

The following outline is an example of an argument developed with a problem-solution outline:

Policy-Argument

Thesis: Commercial television stations should be able to broadcast condom advertisements.

    I.   Sexually transmitted diseases (STDs) are a problem of epidemic proportion in the United States today.

        A.   The results of the problem can be as minor as an infection or as serious as birth defects, sterility, and death.

        B.   The incidence of STDs and the development of new strains of the STDs have increased in recent years.

        C.   Several factors combine to cause the problem.

    II.   Televised commercials for the sale of condoms would help reduce the problem.

        A.   Here is how the solution would work.

        B.   This proposal would reduce the spread of STDs because . . .

Acknowledging the Opposition

As with the value outline, the policy argument can also acknowledge an opposition. If you choose this option, your organization might be like that depicted here.

    I.   Establish a Need
        Use history, examples, case studies, etc.

    II.   Outline a Plan
        Make it as detailed as possible.

    III.   Acknowledge/Refute the Opposition
        Explain any objections.
        Refute them.

    IV.   Proclaim the Practicality of Your Plan
        Stress the solution and added benefits to be gained.

Policy Argument--
Acknowledging and Refuting the Opposition

Thesis: Commercial television stations should be able to broadcast condom advertisements.

I.   The epidemic rate of sexually transmitted diseases in the United States has created a major national problem.

II.   A series of informative television commercials for the sale of condoms would help reduce the problem.

III.   The plan does have its opponents.
    A.   Some religious groups maintain . . .
    B.   However, since the problem has grown steadily for over a decade, a new solution must be sought . . .
    C.   A few parent groups say . . .
    D.   Yet the majority fail to provide teen-agers with enough information early enough to avoid the problem.
    E.   Moreover, commercials can be direct enough to teach, yet not be offensive.

IV.   Television has the power to reach and persuade the teen-age audience.
    A.   Television is a powerful source of information, attitudes, and behaviors for teen-agers.
    B.   Commercials use psychological techniques that appeal to this age group.

V.   Ultimately, condom commercials can be a major force in stopping the epidemic spread of sexually transmitted diseases.

Reflective-Thinking Method

In addition to those patterns already presented, another method has frequently been used in the last 40 years. Called the reflective-thinking method, this pattern is derived from the writing of the American philosopher John Dewey. It has often been used as a method for group problem-solving, but its techniques can be easily applied to your research paper writing. Its main parts are presented here.

I. What is the problem? What is the issue?
- A. Raises the problem as an issue of policy dealing with a law, rule, or course of action, for example: Should forests in the American Northwest be preserved to protect endangered species?
- B. What terms or concepts need to be defined to understand the problem?
- C. How can the problem be defined by numbers and statistics?
- D. What examples can be cited as examples of the problem?

II. What are the causes of the problem?
- A. What are specific causes?
- B. What are specific effects?

III. What are the possible solutions
- A. What criteria must a solution meet?
- B. What possible solutions meet these criteria?

IV. What are the advantages and disadvantages of each solution?

V. What is (are) the best solution(s)?

VI. How can the best solution(s) be put into effect?

Example

I. What is the problem?
- A. Should Columbus State develop a child care facility for the pre-school age children of students, staff and faculty?
- B. _____% of students, staff, and faculty have pre-school age children.
- C. _____ are typical cases of students, staff, and faculty.

II. What are the causes of the problem?
- A. There is a lack of affordable, reliable day care.
- B. Concern over children weakens concentration levels.
- C. Some potential students may not be able to enroll in school.
- D. Poor attendance may result when people must stay home to care for children

III. What are the possible solutions?
- A. Any solution must meet the criteria of affordability, convenience, and state regulations.
- B. Columbus State could provide day care through an independent agency.
- C. Columbus State could establish its own day care program.

IV. What are the advantages and disadvantages of each solution?
- A. Using an independent facility has advantages and disadvantages.
- B. Establishing an in-house child care program has these advantages and disadvantages.

V. What is the best solution?
- A. Columbus State could provide child care through an independent agency.
- B. Columbus State could establish an in-house child care program.

VI. How can the best solution(s) be put into effect?
- A. Federal grants could be sought.
- B. Portable or modular units could be bought to house the program.
- C. The program could serve as a training laboratory for students in the Child Care Technology.

Writing the Argumentative Thesis

As you have seen in the outlines, the main part of the argumentative thesis is the answer to your issue question. At the outset of your work, you may already have a strong opinion and set out to find the evidence that will enable you to defend it. But sometimes you may discover that you cannot support your opinion. The material does not exist or is not available. You may even learn that your opinion was based on faulty assumptions--those gut-level, intuitive ideas you may have but which you have never checked or verified. When this happens, you can change your opinion to accommodate the evidence you find.

Some students have a very difficult time giving up their initial opinion. A few would almost rather change topics than develop a position that they are not emotionally committed to. Try not to let this happen. Avoid topics that lock you in psychologically. Let your research be a voyage to discover material and to form an opinion. The best approach is to be enthusiastic about your topic but to be open to all sides until you have gathered and analyzed your material. You can certainly use some elements of emotion in your essay; however, readers in academic settings respect your conclusions more when they are based on valid material and solid logic.

In phrasing your argumentative thesis, you should follow three guidelines.

1.   State a clear opinion.

In an expository paper, your thesis is a conclusion, an inference, and an objective observation that you make. It often indicates the organization style your essay will use. However, in an argumentative essay, your thesis is a decision, a judgment, and a subjective stand that you take on an issue. It should be clear to your reader what **your** position is. Consider this sentence: **There is a debate about opening the nation's adoption files.** This sentence tells the issue, but it does **not** express the writer's opinion. Notice that the following sentences state clearly the writer's opinion.

Fact: Opening the adoption files would create unwarranted problems for birth parents.

Value: It is undesirable to open the nation's adoption files.

Policy: The nation's adoption files should not be opened.

2. Check for Consistency.

Your thesis should be consistent with your issue question. That is, if you ask a Fact question, you should construct a Fact thesis.

**Fact
Issue:**   Is Chronic Fatigue Syndrome (CFS) a real disease?

**Fact
Thesis:**   Chronic Fatigue Syndrome (CFS) is (not) a real disease.

Similarly, maintain this consistency in the development of your paper. If the purpose announced in your introduction is to defend a fact thesis, sustain that purpose throughout the paper.

Do not admit value arguments. And do not tell the reader what **should** be done.

3. Consider Conditional Vs. Unconditional Statement.

Sometimes you have a very stong opinion on a subject. For you there may be no if's, and's, or but's. At such times you would express an **unconditional** or **unqualified** opinion on the issue. For example:

Further construction of nuclear power plants should be halted.

As it stands, this opinion means **forever;** under no circumstances should another plant be built.

At other times you may have an opinion, but you realize that there could be other conditions, circumstances, or developments, that could change your opinion. For example, how desirable is martial arts training? You might be very enthusiastic about it as a physical and mental fitness activity. However, you recognize that it can be abused if young people do not fully understand its power. Therefore, you might add a **condition** to your statement. For example:

Martial arts training is desirable for children **if they are at least ten years of age**.

Ohio should not develop a high speed rail system **unless business and industry assume the greater share of the cost**.

Conditional statements specify the terms under which you would find an idea or proposal desirable or acceptable. Words like _if_, _until_, _unless_, _providing that_, and _before_ can introduce conditional statements.

For class discussion, consider each of the following policy statements. What conditional statements might you attach to each one.

1. Bungee cord junmping should be permitted in Ohio.

2. Parents should be able to provide home-based eduation for their children.

3. Transracial adoption should be permitted.

4. Employees should be subjected to random drug testing.

5. Mothers receiving AFDC should be required to work or attend school.

A final note:

When assigned an argumentative paper, work with your instructors. See if they have a preferred approach for you to follow. Most are eager for you to be independent in forming your opinion. But some instructors do set their own standards about which argumentative approach to take. Be sure you understand any special requirements of the assignment.

TAKING NOTES

Having defined your purpose and audience and having mapped out a tentative outline, you are ready to find the material you need to develop an explanation of your topic or to construct an argument.

Use your preliminary outline as a checklist for the material you will need. Keep the outline on hand as you read. And constantly question your material. Does it help define your topic? Does it give examples or statistics? Does it help show causes or effects that you want to illustrate? Does it supply support for your argument? If not, you can move to your next source. If it does, you need to take notes.

Form and Techniques for Note Cards

Writers use all kinds of systems for recording information: computers, notebooks, scraps of paper, and index cards. Sometimes your instructor will specify a technique to be used. If not, you can choose for yourself.

Whichever system you use, you must record complete and accurate information. The more methodical your note-taking system is, the more efficiently you will be able to use the notes as you write your paper.

The note card method described here is helpful because it uses a consistent format for recording information. Also, by having notes on separate cards, you can shuffle and rearrange your material to find the best order for the development of your paper.

In general, follow these basic principles:

Use Ink: Pencil smears and fades.

Use Index Cards, One Item Per Card: When notes are on cards, you can easily shuffle and rearrange your material.

Use One Side Of Card Only: Data on the back can be forgotten or ignored.

REQUIRED AND OPTIONAL PARTS

In the note card method, each index card should generally contain **four basic items** of information: (1) the source, (2) the exact page numbers for printed material, (3) a label or "slug" briefly identifying the content, and (4) the note. As the need arises, you may also want to include two additional items: **Attribution Data** and your **Personal Reactions**. All of these items are explained and illustrated below.

1. Source

Identify the source with an abbreviated form--
Author's last name: e.g., **Brodeur**
Author's last name and the first main word of title if you have more than one source by the same author:
  e.g.,   **Brodeur, "Currents"**
          Brodeur, "Hazards"
Use a shortened form of the title if the author is unknown. The title "The Dangers of Electro-magnetic Fields" can be shortened to **"Dangers."**

Use the **first main word** (not "A," "An," or "The") since you will use that word to alphabetize the entry for the "Works Cited."

NOTE: Make it easy to locate the item on your "Works Cited" page.

Don't use the name of a **periodical**. It is very likely that two or more of your sources could come from different issues of the same magazine or newspaper. Identifying material with only the periodical's name will quickly cause confusion.

2. Exact page number(s) for printed material

By recording the page numbers, you can find the location if you need to get further material or to verify the accuracy of a note you have taken. You must also have the page numbers to provide complete documentation as you write your paper.

3.   Label or "Slug"

This label identifies either where you plan to use the material in your paper or what the note contains.

You can more easily sort and arrange a large number of note cards if you include simple labels such as "Introduction," "Definition," "Causes," "Effects," "Benefits," "Solutions," or "Refutation."

Forcing yourself to write these as you take notes also makes you question whether you can use the material at all, and if so, where.

4.   The Note

You may write a paraphrase, a summary, or a direct quotation on your note cards. Sometimes you may even want to record just a statistic or a fragmentary thought.

If you use more than **three consecutive words** from the original, you should consider the citation a direct quotation. Be sure to place Quotation Marks around this material: "   ."

For more on writing summaries and paraphrases, see "Avoiding Plagiarism" pages 30-32.

5.   Attribution Data

For some topics it is very important to take note of **who** said **what, when, where,** and **under what circumstances.** Often you will record the author's credentials on your bibliography cards. But if the author cites someone else, you should also record that person's credentials. You want to show in your paper that you are using reliable sources.

When was a statement made or when was research data released? Identifying a date is very important when you deal with topics in which the information can change over time. For instance, politicians often make promises during a campaign, and once elected, they may follow a different course of action. Also, new scientific and technological data is constantly being reported. By supplying a date, you show that you are reflecting what was known at one specific time.

Where or **under what circumstances** an event occurred or a speech was delivered can be important in helping to explain it. Did it occur in a laboratory under experimental conditions? Or was it an unexplained UFO sighting over a farmer's north forty? Was a speech given to a hostile or receptive audience?

Attribution data is **optional**. But if the topic is very controversial or if the data is changing rapidly, you should take pains to record the dates and any other explanatory information.

6.   Your Reaction

What is your reaction when you read the material?
Do you agree or disagree?
Do you have a comment to add about the article, its content, the   re search, or the public's response to it?

Your reactions are not required. However, by writing them, you force yourself to view your sources more critically. Also, your critical comments help to remind you that your paper should contain some of your own explanations, reactions, and (in argumentation) opinions.**The paper should not be just a stringing together of other people's facts and opinions.**

Many texts recommend enclosing your own reactions in square brackets thus: [   ].

On the following pages you can see sample note cards. Most of the citations come from the sources used in the section called **"Making Bibliography Cards More Useful."** Compare the form and content of a bibliography card with that on a note card.

Sample Note Card—Direct Quotation

	Slug		Source	Page #

	Drug Warning Harvard 17
Quotation	If you are caught using or in possession of illegal drugs, "your government is completely powerless to shield you from the judicial system of a foreign country. Consular officials can only visit the prisoner, provide a list of attorneys, and inform family and friends."
	Material comes from a recent U.S. State Dept. bulletin.
Personal Response	[Young travelers should be encouraged to see the film **Midnight Express** before visiting Europe.]

Sample Note Card—Summary

	Slug	Source	Page #

Summary	Hitch-hiking in Europe Harvard 35 Although hitching can be dangerous, if done carefully it can be an economical, efficient, and interesting mode of transportation. Travelers should keep their belongings in the passenger compartment with them. Women, especially, should use common sense when hitching, traveling in pairs or a woman with a man. Groups of three seldom are successful.
Personal Response	[Readers must be reminded that an extended thumb is not an international sign for hitching. In some countries it is a vulgar insult.]

Sample Note Cards—Two Works By Same Author

Direct Quotation

	Slug	Source	Page #

Quotation	Abuse of Lab Animals Singer, **Animal** 30 "The laboratory rat is an intelligent, gentle animal, the result of many generations of special breeding, and there can be no doubt that the rats are capable of suffering, and do suffer from the countless painful experiments performed on them."
Personal Reaction	[Singer recounts endless gruesome experiments done by the military, industry, and academia.]

Summary

Slug	Source	Page #

Animal Rights Movement	Singer, In Defense	209-10

Summary

The 1980s fired a warning shot heard around the world in defense of animal rights. Following their convictions, activists protested for political support, demonstrated against abusive industries, and broke into laboratories to remove animals being held there. Successes came slowly, but they came. Increased restrictions have been imposed on research with animals. Some tests (especially for cosmetics) have been virtually abandoned. Wildlife has benefited; import bans have stopped the killing of baby seals, and most whale hunting has stopped. Improvements have also been seen in how farmers raise poultry and cattle, and how zoos house animals.

Personal Reaction

[Good outline of what techniques animal rights activists have used and what they have achieved.]

Sample Note Care—Direct Quotation

Slug	Source	Page #

Cleaning Process	Jeffery	697-698

Quotation

Author describes work of Bruno Baratti to clean the Sistine Chapel. "First he wets a natural sponge in distilled, deionized water and gently wipes a small section of fresco. With a natural-bristle brush he applies the cleaning solution. Used by restorers for about 20 years and known as AB 57, it is made of bicarbonates of sodium and ammonium. An antibacterial, antifungal agent is added. All of these are mixed in carboxymethylcellulose and water to become a gel that will cling without dripping."

Attribution Data

Baratti is member of cleaning team under direction of art historian Fabrizio Mancinelli of the Vatican Museums.

Sample Note Card—Paraphrase

Article Has No Author Listed

	Slug	Source	Page #

Paraphrase	Computer Tech. in Film "Taking" 81 Processing Researchers at U of Rochester have developed a computer technique for removing the fuzz from pictures. Working with a computer, they developed a mathematical algorithm that teases information out of blurred pictures and reproduces a clear image. Immediate applications are for aerial and satellite photography.

Sample Note Card—Paraphrase

Source is Personal Interview

	Slug	Source	Page #

	What is "chaos?" Lape. Personal interview.
Summary	"Chaos" is the term to describe the pre-writing confusion that exists in the writer's mind. It includes fuzzy thinking about the topic, purpose, and attitude. It can also include the writer's sense of self-doubt concerning his or her ability to write.
Personal Reaction	[This concept can also be linked to "writer's block" or "writer's anxiety." Are some techniques more helpful than others for breaking the block? How much does the solution depend on the learning style of the student?]

DOCUMENTING SOURCES

When writing a research paper, you are obligated to give credit to others whenever you use their facts, opinions, judgments, organizational structures, and visual aids. Naturally you must use some common sense in deciding what to document. For instance, you need not cite familiar sayings such as "Count your blessings" or well-known quotations like "Neither a borrower nor a lender be." In general, you may consider information that occurs in **five** or more sources general knowledge. The fact that school teacher Christa McAuliffe was killed when the spaceship <u>Challenger</u> exploded need not be documented even if you would record it while reading a book or encyclopedia.

When you have doubts about whether to give credit or not, consult the following list. You should give credit for these citations:

1. **Any** exact wording of three or more consecutive words copied from a source.
2. A summary of original ideas from a source.
3. Factual information taken from a source that is not common knowledge.
4. Any original ideas taken from a source, whether quoted or paraphrased.
5. Phrasing that is distinctive or noteworthy in style, even if it repeats common knowledge.
6. Charts, graphs, tables, and other graphic elements.

MLA Documentation: 1. 2. 3.

Giving credit is called **documenting your sources**. There are many acceptable documentation systems. The **MLA** (Modern Language Association) style described here is used at colleges and universities throughout the country, especially in departments of humanities and the arts. It is acceptable in classes at Columbus State unless your instructor stipulates otherwise. This system uses **parenthetical references** to identify the sources clearly and accurately. Generally the system requires these three parts: (1) the lead-in, (2) the note, and (3) the parenthetical reference.

1. **A Lead-In Device**

This tag signals that the material you are about to give has been borrowed. It prevents your cited material from running together with your own discussion, and thus avoids confusion. There are several types of lead-in devices.

A. **The complete lead-in device: Author & Title**
    Some instructors prefer that you use a complete lead-in device the first time that you borrow from a source. This lead-in includes both the author and title in some combination. For example:

    In <u>Diet for a Small Planet</u>, Frances Moore Lappe argues for vegetarianism as a diet for better health.

    Peter Singer's <u>Animal Liberation</u> criticizes "speciesism"--the attitude people project that says no animals but humans think, create, or feel pain.

B. **Partial lead-in device: Author or Title or Name of Periodical**
    Some instructors prefer that you **always** use a simpler lead-in. And most prefer a simpler tag after you have once used a complete lead-in for a source. This simpler tag can use just the author's last name (if there is only one author with this name in your works cited), or just the title of the book or article, or just the name of the periodical. For example:

    Lappe provides sample vegetarian recipes.

    <u>Animal Liberation</u> illustrates the ways animals have been brutalized on factory farms.

    "The Vegetarian Good Life" explains how one can stay meat-free even when dining in a restaurant.

    According to <u>Prevention</u> magazine, "people who eat vegetarian diets have a lower risk of developing cancer."

C. Generic Lead-in Devices

Some writers use not a specific name or title but a more general term to signal the use of source materials. This lead-in is most effective if it adequately signals that the following material has been borrowed and if the tag is appropriate to your topic. The following are typical generic lead-in devices:

Animal rights advocates maintain . . .
Researchers have discovered . . .
Art critics argue . . .
Historians have concluded . . .
Legal advisors for Planned Parents say . . .

2. The citation

Your borrowed material may be a direct quotation (when you use three or more consecutive words from the original), a summary, or a paraphrase. Sometimes your citation may be a visual aid--a graph, chart, or table that you have borrowed.

3. The parenthetical reference

The parenthetical reference comes at the end of citation and thus tells your reader you are no longer borrowing from the source. What you use in the parenthetical reference depends on how you phrase the lead-in.

The following chart illustrates the basic combinations of lead-in devices and parenthetical notations. The lead-in devices in the left-hand column require the parenthetical notations listed in the right-hand column.

LEAD-IN TECHNIQUE	**PARENTHETICAL REFERENCE**
Author and title or just author in lead-in	**Just page number**

Peter Singer's <u>Animal Liberation</u> argues that   (122-27).
Frances Moore Lappe explains that   (37).
    (28+).

Title, Generic Lead-in, or Name of Periodical	**Author's last name or first main word of title if no author and page number**

<u>Diet for a Small Planet</u> explains   (Lappe 40-42).
"Why I Choose to Veg Out" discusses   (Moore 267).
Vegetarians maintain that   (Shulman 37).
<u>Prevention</u> magazine reports that   ("Vegetarians" 8).
    Source with no author

You have seen the typical elements for documenting a source. Now study several examples which illustrate more completely the variety of documentation possibilities. Remember that references in the text must clearly point to specific sources in the list of works cited. Here is part of a "Works Cited" for a paper on computer crime. As you analyze the techniques for documented sources, note how the sources are related to the entries in the "Works Cited."

Works Cited

Allman, William F. "Computer Hacking Goes on Trial." <u>U. S. News and World Report</u> 22 Jan. 1990: 25.

"Another Infection." <u>Time</u> 12 Dec. 1988: 33.

Bequai, August. <u>How to Prevent Computer Crime: A Guide for Managers</u>. New York: Wiley, 1983.

Hock, Seth A. Personal interview. 15 Jan. 1990.

Morrissey, Jane. "New Security Risks Seen for '90s." <u>PC Week</u> 11 Dec. 1989: 55.

Parker, D. B. "Crime and Computer Security." <u>Encyclopedia of Science and Engineering</u>. 1983 ed.

Stoll, Clifford. <u>The Cuckoo's Egg: Inside the World of Computer Espionage</u>. New York: Doubleday, 1989.

Documentation Samples

1. **A Complete Lead-in uses the author's full name and the title to lead into the borrowed material and requires only the page number(s) of the specific passage in parentheses.**

In <u>How to Prevent Computer Crime</u>, August Bequai estimates that white collar crime costs business and government more than $20 billion yearly (27).

William F. Allman's "Computing Hacking Goes on Trial" defines "cyberpunks" as those computer hackers "who indiscriminately sabotage data" (25).

2. **Once you have used a complete entry for a source, further references to the source can use just the author's last name (for men and women) in the lead-in and the page number in the parenthetical reference.**

Business managers can look to the law enforcement agencies for little help against computer hackers. Bequai says that law enforcement in the United States is "ill-trained and lacking in a cohesive strategy to play an important role in the war against computer crime" (137).

3. **One simplified style is to start the citation with the title of an article or book or the name of the periodical and then include the author's last name and page number in the parenthetical reference.**

    "Computing Hacking Goes on Trial" recounts the story of Robert Morris, the Cornell University graduate, who unleashed a virus that infected thousands of computers across the country (Allman 25).

    How to Prevent Computer Crimes recommends "sign-in logs, badges, authorized entry lists, key lock systems, intruder detection devices, guards, and other related safeguards" as physical measures for deterring hackers (Bequai 198).

    A U. S. News article says that the legal attitude toward computer hackers has gotten more severe with virtually all states passing laws aimed at prosecuting computer crimes (Allman 25).

4. **When you cite the work as a whole rather than a specific section or passage, give the author's name and the title of the work in the lead-in and omit any parenthetical reference.**

    In The Cuckoo's Egg, Clifford Stoll describes his efforts as manager of a Berkeley computer laboratory to track down an unauthorized user of the system.

5. **When you use material from an interview you conduct, lead into it with the name and credentials of the person you interviewed. Notice that the credentials are not a required part of the bibliography form for an interview. Remember to record this information somewhere on the bibliography card for use later. Notice also that for interviews and other non-print sources you use no parenthetical reference.**

According to Seth A. Hock, professor of Computer Science at

Columbus State Community College, a curriculum must develop a sense

of ethical behavior as well as programming competence.

Placing and Punctuating Parenthetical References

To simplify documentation, the MLA style recommends putting the parenthetical reference at the end of the sentence but **before the final period**. Note that if the sentence ends with a direct quotation, the final quotation mark comes **before** the parenthetical reference and that the end punctuation comes **after** the parenthetical reference.

An article in PC Week predicts that "microcomputer theft will escalate

as more criminals realize that the information within the computer is

even more valuable than the hardware" (Morrissey 55).

Sometimes you may need to place the reference **within** your sentence to clarify its relationship to the part of the sentence it documents. In such instances, place the reference at the end of the clause (where a pause would naturally occur) but before the necessary comma.

While Bequai believes that "crime by computer is here to stay" (286),

he exaggerates a bit when he warns that unless a solution is found the

society may experience a new Dark Ages.

When you use a long direct quotation (longer than 4 typed lines), set it off from the main text by indenting it **ten** spaces from the left margin and double-space it. Place the page reference at the end of the passage but **after** the final period. Notice also that there are no **quotation marks** around an indented quotation. The lead-in for a long quotation should be a full grammatical sentence followed by a colon.

Example:

Why is management so reluctant to prosecute computer crimes? One reason, according to Bequai, is that computer hackers are not perceived as especially dangerous:

> The computer criminal is not viewed in the same light as the street criminal. Losses from computer-related crimes are usually passed on by the victim to its customers. However, victims often forget that this mode of behavior ultimately has an impact on the public's perception of the organization. (45)

Special or Unusual Cases

Sometimes you will need to cite sources that are not as straightforward as the examples given above--for example, sources with more than one author, or several sources by the same author. In those cases you will need to modify the standard forms already discussed. The following citations show how to handle eight bibliographical problems that you might encounter. Each example of parenthetical reference is followed by the appropriate entry that would appear in the list of works cited.

1. Citing one work by an author of two or more works

If your list of works cited contains two or more titles by the same author, the least confusing technique is to write a **complete lead-in**; that is, use the author's name and the title in the lead-in.

If you use a generic lead-in, your parenthetical reference will need the author's last name, a comma, a shortened form of the title, and then the relevant page numbers.

Complete lead-in:

Peter Singer's <u>Animal Liberation</u> traces the development of "speciesism" from pre-Christian times to the present (192-222).

Generic lead-in:

Animal rights advocates have suggested several alternatives to experimentation with live animals (Singer, <u>In Defense</u> 83).

Works Cited

Singer, Peter. <u>Animal Liberation: A New Ethics for Our Treatment of Animals</u>. New York: Avon, 1975.

---, ed. <u>In Defense of Animals</u>. New York: Blackwell, 1985.

Special Cases

2. Citing one work by an author who has the same last name as another in your list of works cited

When your list of works cited contains sources by two or more authors with the same last name, avoid confusion by using the author's first and last names in the parenthetical reference **or** in your sentence. In the "Works Cited," the first names of the authors should determine which source is listed first alphabetically.

"An emphasis on testimony, on judgments by one person in a play of the actions or characters of another, has been a basic element of one strain of twentieth century Shakespeare criticism" (Dean Frye 105). Roland Frye notes, "It is quite obvious that the the powers of darkness play an insistent and overt role in <u>Faustus</u>, whereas in <u>Macbeth</u> the demonic is cast in comparatively more ambiguous form" (135).

Works Cited

Frye, Dean. "Commentary in Shakespeare: The Case of Coriolanus." <u>Shakespeare Studies</u>. Ed. J. Leeds Barroll. Cincinnati: Ford, 1965. 105-17.

Frye, Roland M. "Theological and Non-Theological Structures in Tragedy." <u>Shakespeare Studies</u>. Ed. J. Leeds Barroll. Dubuque, IA: Brown, 1968. 132-49.

3.   **Citing a source that is <u>cited within your source</u>**

Often the source you have includes material from an earlier work. What do you do if you want to refer to the earlier work?

To avoid confusion, cite the **original source** in your **lead-in** to the borrowed material. Then indicate the source you are using in the parenthetical reference preceded by the abbreviation **qtd. in** (meaning, **quoted in**) for paraphrases and summaries as well as for direct quotations.

Albert Mehrabian's research in <u>Silent Messages</u> shows that "when a

speaker's body language is inconsistent with his or her words,

listeners tend to believe the body language rather than the words"

(qtd. in Lucas 231).

Works Cited

Lucas, Stephen E. <u>The Art of Public Speaking</u>. 3rd ed. New York:

Random, 1986.

4.   **Citing a work by more than one author**

When citing a work with more than one author, make it clear to your readers. But be careful that you do not clutter your sentence. If you are citing a book by two authors, use both names either in the lead-in or in the parenthetical reference.

If you are citing a book by three or more authors, use just the first author's name plus **et al.** (meaning, "and others") in the parenthetical reference to avoid sentence clutter.

Hanna and Gibson define "credibility" as believability and explain that

it is affected by the speaker's knowledge, trustworthiness, personal

appearance, and extent of audience agreement (295-97).

<u>Public Speaking for Personal Success</u> defines "credibility" as believability and explains that it is affected by the speaker's knowledge, trust-worthiness, personal appearance, and extent of audience agreement (Hanna and Gibson 295-97).

Other communication researchers trace "credibility" back to Aristotle's concept of "ethos" and explain it in terms of competence, sincerity, expertise, friendliness, and dynamism (Ehninger, et al. 343-44).

Note: Usually there is no punctuation between the author's name and the page number. It is required here because **et al. is** an abbreviation.

Works Cited

Ehninger, Douglas, et al. <u>Principles and Types of Speech</u>

<u>Communication</u>. 10th ed. Glenview, IL: Scott, 1986.

Hanna, Michael S., and James W. Gibson. <u>Public Speaking for Personal</u>

<u>Success</u>. Dubuque, IA: Brown, 1987.

5. Citing a Multivolume Work

If your research requires the use of only one volume in a multivolume work, indicate that volume in your list of works cited. If you use all or several of the volumes in writing your paper, document in your parenthetical reference which volume a specific citation comes from.

Critics hostile to modern architecture have misinterpreted Louis Sullivan's familiar slogan "form follows function" (Jordy 3: 85).

Works Cited

Jordy, William H. <u>American Buildings and Their Architects</u>. 3 vols.

New York: Doubleday, 1976.

6. **Citing a work by title**

Alphabetize works by anonymous authors in the list of works cited according to the **first main word** in the title. **Do not alphabetize by "a," "an," or "the."**

Use a short version of the title--or the title itself if it is short--as the first part of the parenthetical reference. Or lead into the borrowed material with the title and use only the page number in the parenthetical reference.

"A commercial anti-viral program called VCHECKER was developed by

American Computer Security" ("Unlucky" 102).

"Unlucky for Some" describes how the computer virus

Datacrime works (100).

Works Cited

"Unlucky for Some." <u>Economist</u> 14 Oct. 1989: 100-02.

7.   Citing a work by a corporate author or government agency

If the author of your source is a corporation or a government agency, you may include the name of the corporation or governmental agency within parentheses, for example: (American Cancer Society 3).   But it is more readable to lead into the borrowed material with the name of the corporate author, especially if you are citing several such reports in your paper.

The American Cancer Society's Why You Should Know About Melanoma explains that "by far the most important known risk factor is excessive exposure to the sun" (3).

In Managing the Common Cold, the American College Health Association recommends single-action cold remedies like pseudophedrine (Sudafed) for congestion, mild antihistamines (Chlor-Trimeton, Dimetane) for runny nose, and cough syrup with an expectorant (Robitussin) for coughs with phlegm (n.p.).

NOTE: n.p. = not paged.   Shorter pamphlets often have no page numbers.   Use the abbreviation n.p. to indicate this.

Works Cited

American Cancer Society.   Why You Should Know About Melanoma.
     1985.

American College Health Association.   Managing the Common Cold.
     Rockville, MD: American College Health Association, 1988.

NOTE: Sometimes pamphlets do not include complete publication data.   The pamphlet from the American Cancer Society does not provide a place of publication or publisher.

8. Citing more than one work in a single parenthetical reference

If you **must** include two or more works in a single parenthetical reference, use a generic lead-in, and then document each reference according to the normal pattern. But separate each citation with a semicolon.

The major speech communication texts identify **competence**, **character**, and **dynamism** as factors in a speaker's credibility (DeVito 43; Lucas 169-170; Verderber 200-201).

Works Cited

DeVito, Joseph A. <u>The Elements of Public Speaking</u>. 3rd ed. New

York: Harper, 1987.

Lucas, Stephen E. <u>The Art of Public Speaking</u>. 2nd ed. New York:

Random, 1986.

Verderber, Rudolph F. <u>The Challenge of Effective Speaking</u>. 4th ed.

Belmont, CA: Wadsworth, 1979.

Note: It **is** possible to cite multiple sources this way, especially to show widespread agreement among authors. But, generally speaking, **you should not do it very often.** Such notes tend to be hard to read and are often repetitive. Save them for those cases where you believe it is imperative to establish that several authorities hold the same opinion.

LEAD-IN DEVICES

The preceding pages give you a variety of ways to handle borrowed material. Most examples include some form of a tag called a **lead-in device**.

Lead-in devices let your readers know that you have borrowed the material you are about to present. They are important because without them, your readers can become easily confused; they cannot tell what is yours and what has been borrowed.

Certainly, there should be little trouble when you are using direct quotations because your quotation marks identify the start of the borrowed material:

> "As franchisers are learning, black entrepreneurs are a committed and resilient group," writes Michael King in Black Enterprise.

However, in some research papers it is difficult to determine what belongs to the writer and what has been borrowed. Especially with paraphrases and summaries, it is often hard to tell how much of the material has been taken from a source. You must use a **parenthetical reference** at the end of the borrowed material. But careless writers often fail to indicate where the material starts. One sentence back? Two? The whole paragraph?

To avoid this confusion, you should learn to use lead-in devices.

In addition to marking the start of borrowed material, lead-in devices can do several other things.

**1.	They identify the source of the material.**

Example:	An article in The New England Journal of Medicine

explains that Harlem has a higher mortality rate for black

men than Bangladesh (McCord and Freeman 173).

2. They help identify the biases, vested interests, and credibility of the source.

How do you respond when you read tabloid headlines that shout, "Big Foot Stole My Wife," "Sunbathing Man Bursts into Flames," or "Mad Organist, 70, Kept Songbird Wife in Cage"? Some people are obviously fascinated by tabloid tales of bizarre behavior or the gossipy stories about the rich and famous. After all, these publications continue to be sold.

However, acting on the principle "consider the source," most people think tabloids are not very reliable sources of information and so have little faith in the truthfulness of their stories.

In a similar way your prior knowledge about a source helps you to interpret information that you receive from it. Through your experience, reading, or often just your intuition you gain an understanding of the biases, vested interests, and credibility of sources.

A **bias** is an identifiable slant or perspective from which a person or publication approaches a story. Kinds of bias include such perspectives as economics, politics, and philosophy. For instance, <u>Ms.</u> magazine has a definite feminist bias while <u>Mother Earth News</u> advocates a philosophy of being self-sufficient and protecting the environment.

A **vested interest** exists when someone has something to gain from a particular outcome of a policy or course of action. For instance, pro-union publications naturally have a pro-worker bias, but the ultimate goal is to keep the workers convinced that the union is doing an effective job representing their concerns to the management.

Credibility means the perceived believability of a source. How reputable is it? When we talk about the credibility of people, we often refer to their educational attainments, experience, accomplishments, and reputation. The credibility of such media as television, magazines, and newspapers rests on their reputation.

What assumptions do you have about the biases, vested interests, and credibility of sources? Try the following experiment.

Imagine that in the following lists the source on the left has been used to provide material for the topic on the right. Can you assume correctly what the position might be? Is your response based on accurate knowledge about the source's bias, vested interest, or credibility? Or is it just a hunch? If it is just a hunch, how accurate is it? Discuss your responses in class.

Lead-ins

SOURCES	TOPICS
Field and Stream	gun control
Ms.	abortion
John Molloy, author of Dress for Success	men wearing an earring for a job interview
Columbus Dispatch	national politics
Watch Tower	creationism in the schools
Christian Science Monitor	analysis of world events
Consumer Reports	buying a new car

3. **They can provide interpretive hints to tell your readers what kind of tone or position you detect in the source.**

As the writer of the research paper, you should not just give readers material to interpret for themselves. Instead, you should help them to understand what it means. What is the author doing? Attacking a current policy? Proposing a new policy? Presenting the results of a research experiment?

Also, what **tone** do you detect in the sources you read? You should share this with your readers.

Examples: Jessica Mitford's The American Way of Death **attacks** sales strategies used by the nation's funeral directors.

In "Improving Monetary Policy," Milton Friedman **outlines** major economic changes that must be made.

Jacob Weisberg in "Gays in Arms" **argues** for the right of homosexuals to serve in the nation's armed forces.

Notice that each of the highlighted words has a slightly different degree of emotional stress. "Attack" is obviously more forceful than a moderate word like "outline." And "argue" identifies the persuasive purpose of the article.

Interpretive words like these help you to guide your readers' understanding of the material you present. More words are given later under "Interpretive Vocabulary."

What to Include in Lead-In Devices

Use the Attribution Data you recorded on your note cards. (See "Taking Notes" pages 144-151.) Who said it? When? Where? To whom? Under what conditions? Answer **only** those questions that will help build credibility in your paper.

Names: Will educated readers recognize it?

Positions of Writers: Is it a position of responsibility?
What is the job title?
Does the place have high name recognition or status?

Credentials of Writers: What academic degrees does the writer have?
What awards has the writer received?

Use some common sense when deciding when to add credentials. Not all lead-ins need them. Provide the writer's position or credentials **only** if the information helps to enhance the source's credibility. Do this when the material is distinctive. For instance, virtually every writer in a professional legal journal would have a law degree. It would not be necessary to mention the writer's law degree in a lead-in device.

Also, avoid providing obvious or well-known information. It too often becomes mere padding. For example:

Reader's Digest, a popular magazine that appears in 15 languages and sells 25 million copies a month, reports that . . .

Adult readers should already know this!

Developing Skill with Lead-In Devices

Better writers not only inform their readers with carefully documented materials, but they also do it with a stylistic flare to make the writing interesting.

You can start developing your own stylistic techniques by practicing a few tricks when writing lead-in devices. These tricks include (1) varying the kinds and completeness of lead-in devices, and (2) using interpretive vocabulary.

Adding Variety

To vary the kind and completeness, you might write a **complete lead-in** the first time you use a source. Keep an eye on readability; if the lead-in is long and awkward you might try a shorter variation.

Examples: In Dress for Success, John Molloy recommends . . .

In her Newsweek column, Meg Greenfield advocates . . .

Use the complete lead-in only once. From then on whenever you refer to that source, use just the author's last name, or if there is no author, use a short form of the title. Note that it is now correct to use the last name only for women also.

Examples: As for short sleeve shirts for business, Molloy criticizes . . .

Greenfield believes that all sides in the environmental debate have credibility problems.

Using Interpretive Vocabulary

Too often beginning writers grab onto one kind of lead-in device (Usually "**According to . . .** " or So-and-so "**says**" or "**states**") and want to use it whenever they cite material.

Three things are wrong with this practice:

1. These lead-ins do nothing to help your readers understand the material.

2. Expressions like "According to . . ." and verbs like "say" or "state" make the reader think you have accepted your source completely without bothering to criticize or analyze the facts or judgments being given.

3. They are boring! Reading them more than a couple of times in a short paper is tiresome.

You can help your readers by using lead-in devices that explain and interpret the material.

Decide what the authors of your sources are doing and indicate that in your lead-in device. The following list contains some words that will help show what your material might be doing. The words in each group carry a variety of connotations--emotional responses. Select the word that carries the most appropriate tone and level of stress. Room has been left to include your own terms.

STATE: say, tell, maintain, declare, express, recount, narrate, set forth, present, explain, report, describe, expound

QUESTION: ask, inquire, examine, probe, interrogate, quiz, sound out, grill, test, drill,

ANSWER: respond, reply, retort, react to

EXPLAIN: describe, demonstrate, make clear, make plain, illustrate, illuminate

JUDGE (NEGATIVE): blame, attack, condemn, criticize, assail, vilify

JUDGE (POSITIVE): praise, endorse, support, verify, applaud, commend

GUESS: speculate, estimate, theorize, assume, hypothesize, postulate

PLAN: organize, devise, conceive, plot, design, outline, project, map out, diagram, propose, sketch, list

COMPLAIN: criticize, carp, cavil, grumble, grouse

A final note:

Use some common sense with these expressions. Not all synonyms for a term are interchangeable. Consult a dictionary for their literal and emotional meanings. The right word can create a strong impact on your readers. The wrong word can confuse them, make them think you are pompous, or--even worse--make them laugh when you have no intention of being funny. Mark Twain once wrote that the difference between the right word and the almost right word is the difference between lightning and a lightning bug. Try to find the "right" word.

The following is a sample expository paper that was originally prepared for an Essay and Research class. It has been fully annotated so that you can better see what the parts are, where they belong, and how they work together.

The following comments explain the form of the research paper and explain specific problems you may encounter.

Notice that the title page consists of three parts: the title, student data, and course information. Double-space each unit.

Place the title approximately one third down the page.

Write your name with "by" on separate lines.

Include the course name and number, instructor's name and date submitted.

Note: The pages have been enclosed in boxes to simulate the layout on a page of text. Obviously, margins and layout are not to scale. Plan at least a one inch margin on all sides of your paper.

Operating a Successful Bed and Breakfast

by

Luanna J. Klaiber

Essay and Research 1003

Mrs. Newton

November 3, 19xx

Plan your page layout to have at least a one inch margin on all sides. Place your last name and page number in the upper right-hand corner, a half inch from the top.

Note the use of a small Roman numeral i for this introductory page.

The thesis statement names the subject of the paper and indicates what direction the development will take.

The main points of the outline are presented as questions. The student could also have used declarative sentences or phrases. Notice that sometimes she has chosen to use the questions as topic sentences, and sometimes she has changed them to declarative sentences for stylistic variety.

The outline is double-spaced throughout.

The conclusion here is word-for-word as it appears at the end of the paper. You may also summarize your conclusion, omitting any borrowed material.

Outline

<u>Thesis statement</u>: Before opening their doors to guests, prospective hosts need to understand the nature of the business and to follow some helpful advice offered by other hosts and consultants in the business.

1.   What is a bed and breakfast?

2.   How has the bed and breakfast industry evolved in this country?

3.   What legal issues need to be researched by prospective bed and breakfast hosts?

4.   Are there certain requirements regarding accommodations in bed and breakfasts?

5.   How are bed and breakfast room rates determined?

6.   What should hosts plan to serve for breakfast?

7.   Are there any associations or other supporting agencies to assist bed and breakfast hosts?

Conclusion: Operating a successful bed and breakfast obviously involves more than filling up some empty space in a large old home. Hosts must be willing to research carefully and plan before opening their doors to strangers. The best hosts make strangers feel genuinely welcome by offering them clean, comfortable accommodations and a good breakfast. Finally, hosts must make use of networking groups, reservation service organizations, and other supporting agencies capable of promoting the bed and breakfast industry.

The student uses MLA Style for format, parenthetical references, and Works Cited.

Page number. Since the student used a cover page, she typed the number 1 in the upper right-hand corner, placed a half inch from the top edge. On the following pages, she typed the page number preceded by her last name.

Title. The title prepares the reader for the paper in two ways; it states the topic of the essay (bed and breakfasts), and it focuses the topic (operating these home businesses). Note that the title on page one is exactly as it appears on the title page. After the title triple or quadruple-space before starting paragraph one.

Introductory device. The student uses a long quotation, announces the topic, narrows it, and leads into the thesis statement. Other introductory devices include examples, definitions, quotations, statistics, questions, and startling statements.

Notice that the introductory device has complete documentation: a lead-in device, the quotation, and a parenthetical reference. Note the abbreviation **qtd. in** before the author's name. This means the author is citing the passage from a previously published work.

The student's note card looked like the one below.

Myth v. Reality/   Stankus, Foreword ix
Use in Intro.

"Bed and breakfast hosting seems like the most natural home
occupation in the world . . . and it really is. On first thought,
one would think that anyone who has managed a home, enter-
tained guests, or chatted with strangers at a social gathering
could become a successful B&B host without any further training.
Those of us in the business know that his is not quite true."

Arline Kardasis, membership chairman, Bed and Breakfast,
The National Network

1

Operating a Successful Bed and Breakfast

Running a bed and breakfast is not as easy as it looks,
according to Arline Kardasis, membership chairperson of Bed
and Breakfast, The National Network:

> Bed and breakfast hosting seems like the most
>
> natural home occupation in the world . . . and it
>
> really is. On first thought, one would think that
>
> anyone who has managed a home, entertained
>
> guests, or chatted with strangers . . . could become a
>
> successful B&B host without further training. Those
>
> of us in the business know that this is not quite
>
> true. (qtd. in Stankus ix)

An increasing number of people are contemplating opening bed
and breakfasts on farms, in cities, and around popular tourist
sites. However, before opening their doors to guests, prospective
hosts need to understand the nature of the business and to follow
some some helpful advice offered by other hosts and consultants in
the industry.

Topic sentence. Notice that the student has used the question from her outline as the topic sentence for the definition paragraph.

What is a B&B?   Stankus xi-xii

"Inns are small commercial enterprises (usually having four to twelve guest rooms) in which breakfast is usually part of the deal, just as it is in a bed and breakfast home. But a bed and breakfast home is in a class by itself."

"A bed and breakfast home is a private residence or other structure on a homeowner's property (such as a guest house or cabin) that is used to accommodate paying guests overnight. Breakfast (either continental or full) is provided.

Example of B&B Owner   Preston 58-59

58
Jerry Rowan had been a sales representative for the Du Pont Corporation for 40 years. After his wife died, he was alone in a 150-year-old farmhouse about one hour's drive southwest of Philadelphia.

59
Rowan heard about a woman who was starting a reservation service for bed and breakfasts. Jerry signed up and ever since he has had a steady flow of customers.

Klaiber 2

What is a bed and breakfast? Bed and breakfasts are often

confused with country inns. In her book, <u>How to Open and

Operate a Bed and a Breakfast Home</u>, Jan Stankus clarifies the

distinction. Country inns are commercialized enterprises usually

consisting of several guest rooms where breakfast is served as a

<u>part</u> of the package, but generally three meals a day are served.

The bed and breakfast home, on the other hand, "is a private

residence or other structure on a homeowner's property (such

as a guest house or cabin) that is used to accommodate paying

guests overnight" (xii). Usually bed and breakfasts are run by

ordinary homeowners who happen to have couple of spare

bedrooms. In a <u>Country Journal</u> article, Richard Preston shares

a typical example of how bed and breakfast hosts get started in

the business. At age 62, Jerry Rowan, a retired widower, found

himself living alone in a large 150-year-old farmhouse about an

hour's drive southwest of Philadelphia. He contacted a woman in

the area who had started a reservation service for bed and

breakfast homes. After meeting with her and deciding that he

met her qualifications, he registered his home with the service

Topic sentence. Here the student has turned the question into a declarative sentence. Doing so helps create some stylistic variety in the paper.

Origin and Evolution   Fossel 39

"Bed-and-breakfasts have for generations been a favorite and traditional type of lodging place for European travelers, especially in Britain; and while an estimated 10,000 such accommodations exist in this country, with another 1,500 or so being established every year, the concept is still new enough here that not everybody knows yet what a bed-and-breakfast is—let alone how to find a good one."

and began renting out two guest rooms on the third floor of his house. Since then, he has had a steady stream of paying guests (58-59).

The bed and breakfast industry in this country got a relatively late start. Only in the last decade has this form of household enterprise had significant growth in the United States. But in Europe, according to Peter Fossel's "B&Bs Today," this has been a favorite and traditional type of lodging for generations (39). Americans abroad enjoyed this more relaxed, homelike mode of travel. And they discovered that they did not have to stay in luxury hotels and pay the high rates associated with them. Most important, Americans were inspired to start their own bed and breakfast businesses. Today, Fossel estimates that there are over 10,000 bed and breakfasts in the United States with 1,500 being established each year (39).

As with any new business, bed and breakfasts raise several legal issues such as zoning laws, health and safety regulations, and tax consequences. In "Starting Your Own Little Country Inn," Robert Kaldenbach points out that the bed and breakfast

Legal issues   Kaldenbach 108

"Do zoning regulations permit you to operate a B&B in your
neighborhood? Is it legal for you to serve meals to your guests?
Because B&B is yet so young in America, most communities do not have
ordinances to regulate them."

Legal issues   Stankus 226

"It's possible that you will need to obtain a variance or go before a zoning
board hearing. The board will be interested in how much hosting you
plan to do and whether the activity will disturb the neighborhood in any
way—such as causing noise or parking problems. Be ready to distinguish
your B&B from a 'rooming house' that accommodates 'tenants,' as there
may be a precedent excluding boarding houses, inns, hotels, or motels
from residential areas. . . ."

"As a bed and breakfast host, you are of course concerned about the
safety and well-being of your guests, just as you are about that of your
family . . . . A host's concerns about possible fire, theft, personal injury,
or property damage should take two forms—prevention and insurance."

Legal issues: keeping records   Stankus 235

". . . managers of reservation service organizations across North America
were asked to identify the three biggest mistakes made by new B&B hosts.
Nancy Jenkins, manager of the Bed & Breakfast Exchange in St. Helena,
California, said this: 'Not being well enough prepared for the bookkeeping and accounting aspects of the business.'"

industry is still so young in this country that many communities
do not have ordinances governing their operation (108).
Stankus provides the following advice to people living in areas
where the laws have not been changed to permit B&Bs:

> Be ready to distinguish your bed and breakfast from a
> "rooming house" that accommodates "tenants," as
> there may be a precedent excluding boarding
> houses, inns, hotels, or motels from residential
> areas . . . . A host's concerns about possible fire,
> theft, personal injury, or property damage should
> take two forms—prevention and insurance. (226)

It is very important to remember that income generated by
hosting is subject to taxes and must be accounted for. It is,
therefore, essential to keep accurate records. When managers of
reservation service organizations were asked to pinpoint the
biggest mistake made by new hosts, Nancy Jenkins, manager of
the Bed & Breakfast Exchange in St. Helena, California,
answered, "Not being well enough prepared for the bookkeeping
and accounting aspects of the business" (Stankus 235). Owners

Legal issues: keeping records   Preston 60-61

Whether you are renting out just a couple of spare bedrooms or turning your whole house into a bed and breakfast, you must be careful to maintain accurate records. The best approach is to contact a tax lawyer or accountant who can work out an efficient means of bookkeeping.

should keep a guest register, as well as a record of daily operational expenses such as office supplies, food, utilities, and advertising. Also, since the spare rooms are used as a principal place of business, many of these expenses may be tax-deductible. Preston recommends working with a tax expert to set up a system of bookkeeping and recording one's expenses (60-61).

Are there certain requirements regarding accommodations in bed and breakfasts? Although there are no government regulations for bed and breakfasts in the United States, there is general agreement among reservation service organizations about what basics should be provided in any B&B. In her book, Stankus lists and discusses these in detail. It is sufficient here just to outline the "basics." The essential furnishings for the bedroom should include a bed of the highest quality (sturdy, firm mattress), an easy chair, night table, reading lamp and mirror. Other items considered "basics" and appreciated by guests are an alarm clock, extra blankets, facial tissue, luggage rack, and a privacy lock on the door. For the bathroom, which need not be private, the most important

Basic Requirements   Stankus 50-74

50-60 Bedroom: a good bed of the highest quality, a "firm" mattress (gives information for judging the quality), an easy chair, night table, reading lamp, mirror, alarm clock, extra blankets, facial tissue, luggage rack, privacy lock on the door

60-65 Bathroom: plumbing in good working order, an adequate supply of cold and hot water, non-skid rugs and bath mats, a grip rail for the tub, a privacy lock for the door, adequate supply of bath towels, wastebasket, drying rack, shelf space for toiletries, hooks for robes, soap, toilet tissue, water glass

66-74 Amenities: fresh flowers, fruit, candy, wine, reading materials, games, television, VCR, radio, kitchen privileges.

Room rates   Kaldenbach 108

"Call up every cheap motel, guesthouse, and B&B on your first list and ask the one-night rate for a room with a double bed, with and without private bath. Now you know the prevailing lowest room rates for your area. Write down the rates as you learn them beside the names on the competition list."

Klaiber 6

concern should be that the plumbing is in good working order and that there is an adequate supply of cold and hot water. For the safety of guests, it is advisable to provide non-skid rugs and bath mats, a grip rail for the tub, and a privacy lock for the door. Other basics would include an adequate supply of towels, wastebasket, drying rack, shelf space for toiletries, hooks for robes, soap, toilet tissue, and one water glass per guest. While accommodations need only have the "basics," any amenities or extras provided by hosts are what make the bed and breakfast experience special for guests. Extras may include such items as fresh flowers, fruit, candy, wine, reading materials, games, television, VCR, radio, and kitchen privileges (50-74).

Room rates in B&Bs are based on several factors. The location of the home, amenities provided, and national averages are just three elements. A simpler approach, according to one writer, is for hosts to price their rooms at a rate comparable to lower priced hotels or motels in an area (Kaldenbach 108). In an interview Glen and Beverly Schmidt, operators of Bloom Village Inn, Lithopolis, Ohio, were asked how they had

Room rates   Schmidt. Personal interview.

Glen Schmidt said he contacted several moderately priced "no frills" motels in their area. He used their prices for determining how much he and his wife would charge per night for their rooms. Glen and Beverly will also deal with guests; if the guests stay more than three nights they get a better rate. The price also varies according to if the room has a private bath or if the guest must share a bathroom with other guests.

Room rates   Stankus 76-77

"The survey shows that the average price range for a single room is $27-56, with the overall average price $40 . . . . The average price range for a double identified by survey results is $35-$82, with the overall average price $50." "Before guests make reservations at a bed and breakfast, they usually shop around to see what's available for the best price."

Breakfast foods   Schmidt. Personal interview.

Originally the Schmidts wanted to serve a full breakfast. However, they discovered that as soon as they had served a maximum of five full meals, they would have to meet some strict health department regulations. So they chose to offer a continental breakfast.

determined their room rates. Glen stated that he had called several moderately priced, "no frills" motels in his area, and used their rates as a guideline for determining what he and Beverly would charge. The Schmidts' bed and breakfast also offers varying rates based on occupancy, whether or not the room has private bath, and the length of stay. Stankus' book contains the results of a survey of 125 hosts and reservation service organizations across the country; from that survey the "average price range for a single room is $27-$56, with the overall average price being $40 . . . . The average price range for a double is $35-82, with the overall average price being $50." Most guests will shop for the best accommodations at the most affordable price (76-77).

What should hosts plan to serve for breakfast? The morning meal is usually one of two types in these establishments: either a continental breakfast or a full breakfast. A continental breakfast usually consists of coffee, juice, pastries, and fresh fruit. The Schmidts, for example, opted to serve the continental breakfast after learning that they were allowed to

Breakfast food   Kaldenbach 111

"Breakfast is extreme in its importance to B&B guests, far more so than just the calories that are consumed. Breakfast is the one chance the guest has to get at you, to gain information from a local, a townie, someone who knows things they don't know. The fare can be as modest as juice, toast, and coffee, or as grand as the hosts of Ireland serve, exceeding even the "country breakfasts" of old America. Over there its eggs, meat, homemade bread, tea, potatoes, and more." "In our experience, the guests will eat up almost anything within reach and in sizable quantities."

serve only a maximum of five full guest meals in their home
without meeting some strict health department regulations. At
other B&Bs, breakfast is a fancy course meal, a traditional
country breakfast, or the "specialty of the house." For instance,
in Niagara-on-the-Lake, Canada, Karl and Dietlinda Witt, natives
of Prussia, advertise a "full German breakfast." This includes
meats, eggs, fresh fruit and vegetables from their garden, as well
as Mrs. Witt's homemade marmalade and breads. But B&B
guests are often less fussy about food than other travelers. "In
our experience," shares Kaldenbach, "the guests will eat up
almost anything within reach and in sizable quantities" (111).

Although the bed and breakfast industry is fairly young in
this country, there is already a wealth of support available to
hosts. Groups such as Helping Hands, an informal network of
hosts across the United States, answer questions from new hosts
and give them advice based upon their personal experience.
Reservation service organizations (RSOs) make bookings for
guests in bed and breakfasts. A host pays a membership fee plus

Associations   "Bed and Breakfast" 5-6 C

Ohio's bed and breakfast industry counts more than 200 B&Bs statewide
and is organizing itself into an association.

The 97 association members will publish a directory early next year.
The association will provide information on what's available in Ohio.

Training seminars   McLaughlin 10

Margaret Lobenstine, proprietor of the Wildwood Inn in Ware, Mass., has
operated successfully for 10 years. For 14 weeks every year, she closes her
inn to regular guests and runs it as a week-long school for potential
B&Bers. Classes are limited to 10 students who get "hands-on" experience
regarding the operation of a bed and breakfast. Lobenstine covers such
subjects as location, clientele, building, publicity, food, and finances.

Klaiber 9

a commission for each guest referred through the booking
service.

In some states associations have been created to assist
hosts in promoting their bed and breakfast business. A recent
column in The Columbus Dispatch, says that bed and breakfasts
are the fastest growing segment of the Ohio accommodations
industry. This rapid growth has led to the creation of the Ohio
Bed and Breakfast Association consisting of 97 members whose
purpose is to provide information about what bed and breakfasts
are available in their state ("Bed and Breakfast" 5-6 C).

Educational seminars are also available to those who want
to learn more about running a bed and breakfast. Mary
Lobenstine, owner of the Wildwood Inn in Ware, Massachusetts,
closes her business to outside guests for 14 weeks every year,
and opens it as a school for prospective bread and breakfast
hosts. Classes are limited to 10 students who not only receive
"hands-on" experience regarding the operation of a bed and
breakfast, but also cover such subjects as location, clientele,
publicity, food, and finances (McLaughlin 10).

The concluding paragraph here is the same as it appears in the outline. If the conclusion is longer, it could be summarized for the outline.

Klaiber 10

Operating a successful bed and breakfast obviously involves more than filling up some empty space in a large old home. Hosts must be willing to research carefully and plan before opening their doors to strangers. The best hosts make strangers feel genuinely welcome by offering them clean, comfortable accommodations and a good breakfast. Finally, hosts must make use of networking groups, reservation service organizations, and other supporting agencies capable of promoting the bed and breakfast industry.

Bibliography. Called a "Works Cited," this section follows MLA documentation style. Entries are in alphabetical order by author's last name or first main work of title (if no author is given), with a 5-space indentation after the first line of each entry. Punctuation and spacing between words and lines are as indicated. Double-space within and between entries. Two spaces occur after periods that conclude a section; one space after abbreviations. One space after colons.

Works Cited

"Bed and Breakfast, an Industry Waking Up in Ohio." <u>Columbus</u>

<u>Dispatch</u> 15 Oct. 1989: 5-6 C.

Fossel, Peter V. "B&Bs Today: What to Expect, How to Choose."

<u>Country Journal</u> Apr. 1988: 39.

Kaldenbach, Robert. "Starting Your Own Little Country Inn."

<u>Yankee</u> May 1984: 104-112.

McLaughlin, Charles. "To B&B or Not to B&B." <u>New Choices for</u>

<u>the Best Years</u> Mar. 1989: 10-11.

Preston, Richard M. "Bed and Breakfast." <u>Blair and Ketchem's</u>

<u>Country Journal</u> June 1984: 58-63.

Schmidt, Glen, and Beverly Schmidt. Personal interview.

21 Oct. 1989.

Stankus, Jan. <u>How to Open and Operate a Bed & Breakfast</u>

<u>Home</u>. Chester, CT: Globe, 1986.

Witt, Karl, and Dietlinda Witt. Personal interview. 14 Nov. 1989.

The following is a sample argumentative paper that was written for an Essay and Research class. This paper focuses on an issue of value: How desirable is it for married men to assume the role of househusbands?

As you read the paper, notice how it is organized and how the source material has been incorporated to support the main points. Notice also that the student has included some of his own comments and explanations.

Remember, the pages have been boxed to simulate a page layout. Your pages should have at least a one-inch margin on all sides.

Househusbands: A Good Choice

by

Donny L. Taylor

Essay and Research 1003

Dr. Ehret

September 5, 19xx

Outline

<u>Thesis</u> <u>Statement</u>: Even though men who choose to stay home and take care of the house and children often receive criticism from others, becoming a househusband can be a desirable lifestyle choice.

1. Househusbands often receive criticism from other men who feel that a man's place is in the workforce, not in the home.

2. Some people think that househusbands are not as good at doing housework and providing childcare as women.

3. Yet men who become househusbands are given the chance to act like children again, and get away with it.

4. Househusbands give their wives the opportunity to pursue their own careers.

5. By becoming househusbands, men have the opportunity to spend more quality time with their children.

6. As househusbands, men realize that some things are more important than money.

7. Househusbands can often provide children better care than they can receive from a day care center or private sitter.

8. Studies show that when men are househusbands their children tend to be better developed socially.

<u>Conclusion</u>: As more men decide to stay home and become househusbands, they will realize the benefits they are providing for their children as well as the personal satisfaction they receive from the time spent with their children. This will lead more and more men to consider being househusbands as a viable, if not preferred option. Thus, househusbands will become more commonplace--maybe even considered a norm. But this social change cannot occur without understanding and support from others. For, as Straus states, "This househusbandry . . . requires courage, sacrifice and a resilient ego, and men who accept its challenges need support--from societal institutions, other men, and particularly from women who, after all, have been there before" (71).

Househusbands: A Good Choice

Today, many married men are getting a major life style choice:
go into the work force or stay at home with the children. Men who
make the choice of staying at home with the children often must face
much opposition. According to a Randall Beach's Utne Reader article,
"househusbands, even in this liberated age, are frequently asked
'Don't you feel inadequate?' . . . 'Can't you hack it in the workforce'"
(Beach 79)? And there is still the question of whether men can do as
good of a job at housekeeping and childcare as women. In "Make
Room for Daddy!" David Laskin describes one househusband as ". . . not
overly thrilled about doing housework, [but who] loves the close
relationship he has with his children as a result of the time he spends
with them. 'I really know my kids,' he says proudly" (185). Even
though men who become househusbands receive criticism from
others, becoming a househusband is a desirable move.

Househusbands often receive criticism from other men who feel
that a man's place is in the workforce, not in the home. They feel that
men who become househusbands cannot "hack it" in the workforce.
In Randall Beach's article, one househusband stated that he "received
some interesting reactions from his male friends: 'Do you really know
what you're doing?' and 'Keep it quiet: if women hear about this,

they'll want more of us to do it'" (81).

Some people think that househusbands are not as good at doing housework and providing childcare as women. Katherine Karlsrud explains in "Helping Dads Help Out" that most men are not completely comfortable with their participation in baby care. This is due in part to awkwardness or some hesitancy toward providing this care. Why? Most men did not have fathers in such active roles when they were children (200).

Admittedly, there are numerous reasons why a man might not want to become a househusband. However, there are many more reasons why men could consider being a househusband as a positive lifestyle choice.

First, men who become househusbands are given the chance to act like children and get away with it. Fathers play games with their children and can pretend to be a child again themselves. Many times fathers can play the games they played as a kid, or they can live out their own dreams (once held as a child--the star baseball player, or the fastest gun in the west) with and through their children. In the guise of entertaining the children, fathers can act silly and have

Taylor 3

"fun" without taking the risk that adults find them childish or immature. If a man was seen jumping rope and hopping down the street singing songs, someone would probably call the guys with little white jackets to come take him away. However, when a man does this sort of activity while accompanied by a child, people stop and admire or even envy him. A child is so carefree and the adult who plays with that child can forget the responsibilities of this hectic world if only for a short time. In "Freaks of Nurture" Hal Straus tells of one man's experience: "The awareness my children bring to me every day is incredible . . . from noticing the small animals in the park to smelling the flowers. I could spend years meditating on the here and now--my son dwells there and brings that into my life" (71).

Second, househusbands give their wives the opportunity to pursue their own careers. Many women are now putting their careers first and becoming very successful. Women who have children are often faced with the possibility of putting their career on hold until the child reaches school age. Men who choose to stay at home with the kids during the preschool years give their wives the opportunity to continue in their chosen career without worrying about the quality of care given to their children. Today many women are earning salaries greater than their spouses, and it is difficult for the family to live on the lower income. Thus the decision is often primarily a financial one.

Taylor 4

Barbara Goldberg's "More Dads Stay Home With Kids as Wife Works" explains that while for some families Mom working and Dad staying at home is purely an economic equation, other families find it a way to satisfy personal needs. Some women are not interested in staying at home; they want to get back into their careers as quickly as possible (6B).

Equally important, by becoming househusbands men have the opportunity to spend more quality time with their children. However, just their presence in the home does not guarantee quality time. Beach cites the opinion of quality time from one man who says, "that's bogus. You can't just show up and say 'O.K., I'm here to give you quality time." [The kids] might be ready to take a nap" (82). Men who work outside the home often do not have time or energy to spend with their children. Househusbands are able to dedicate a large portion of their day to the needs and development of their children. Certainly, the men who come home after a hard day at work can receive the love and attention of their children. However, the time they actually spend together is quite limited. The children must eat, take baths, and get to bed early. The men need to relax and unwind, eat and get rested in preparation for the next day. This allows very little time needed to meet other social commitments let alone spend "quality time" with children. Househusbands, on the other hand, have this time for the spontaneous love and affection that children give and receive.

Furthermore, as househusbands men realize that some things are more important than money. There are more important issues at hand, such as the welfare of the children. Making the choice of one parent staying at home when both may have worked prior to having children means some financial sacrifice. Men are making the choice of staying at home to provide a parent's love and care to their children instead of working outside the family to provide more material things. Typically when both wife and husband work full time they can increasematerial comforts in their lives. New cars, clothes, and vacations can become realities. However, time and togetherness are two things the added money cannot buy. For many couples children cause a shift in values from acquiring goods to improving the overall quality of one's life and relationships. Spending time with the children becomes a top priority. In the Utne Reader, Beach gives the description of some sentiments about sacrifice: "Men have a hunger for warm relationships. They've found that the BMW and condo are not what life is truly about" (82).

Besides, househusbands can often provide their children better care than they can receive from a day care center or private sitter. Children are very vulnerable and dependent upon their parents to provide them with a safe, healthy, and loving environment to grow and develop. Finding quality care for a child while both parents work is both difficult and expensive. Many couples find themselves in a dilemma; they do not feel comfortable allowing a stranger or mere acquaintance to provide care for their child. Thus they must make a difficult decision - Who? In "One Man and a Little Lady: A Dad Stays Home," Robert Baker talks of one couple's dilemma: "Our little family faced some questions, routine ones today for two-income couples: Would we hand over our bundle of unblemished hope to a day care center? Or to a babysitter? Neither seemed right" (91). Goldberg states that parents often do not wish to send their children to day care, so they decide that one parent will stay at home. "Why should it matter which parent?" Once the baby is here, that question gets tough (6B). More men today are deciding that they will be the one to stay at home and provide the love and care their child needs and deserves. Goldberg cites statistics that show the number of househusbands has increased by 267% in the last two decades (6B).

Finally, studies show that their children tend to be better developed socially. Mothers and their children form a close, intimate relationship built on dependency. From the first moment of birth a child is dependent upon its mother for survival. Mother nature intended it this way. However, fathers can provide children with an environment that allows each child to develop his/her own sense of identity. Fathers tend to play rougher with their children than mothers do. In "The Father Factor" by Carla Cantor, James A. Levine describes these research findings: "Fathers help children forge an identity outside the powerful intimacy of the mother-child relationship" (40). Having been a househusband for three years, I have had the opportunity to observe other children as well as my own. It is interesting to see how differently children behave and develop when the father works outside the home or is totally absent. With little or no contact with male role models, children often have problems relating to men and sometimes completely ignore the authority of men when they are corrected or given instruction. One little girl at my child's pre-school is an interesting case. She is three, the same age as my daughter, but lives in a single-parent home with her mother. She is shy and timid when around adults and also is much slower in her development. For example, she is not potty trained, she speaks very haltingly, and is not as developed socially as other children her age. Admittedly, it is very difficulty to compare children because each develops at his/her own pace, yet it appears that children who spend more time with their fathers often develop quicker and have more self-confidence. Carla Cantor lists confidence and flexibility as two of the positive traits children develop when they spend a great deal of time with their fathers (40).

As more men decide to stay at home and become house-husbands, they will realize the benefits they are providing for their children as well as the personal satisfaction they receive from the time spent with their children. This will lead more and more men to consider being househusbands as a viable, if not preferred, option. Thus, househusbands will become more commonplace--maybe even considered a norm. But this social change cannot occur without understanding and support from others. For, as Straus states, "This househusbandry . . . requires courage, sacrifice and a resilient ego, and men who accept its challenges need support--from societal institutions, other men, and particularly from women who, after all, have been there before" (71).

Taylor 9

Works Cited

Barker, Robert. "One Man and a Little Lady: A Dad Stays Home."
Business Week 15 Apr. 1991: 91.

Beach, Randall. "Househusbands: Stay-at-home Men Are Still Few in
Number." Utne Reader Mar. - Apr. 1990: 79-82.

Cantor, Carla. "The Father Factor." Working Mother June 1991:
39-42 + 44.

Goldberg, Barbara. "More Dads Stay Home with Kids as Wife Works."
Columbus Dispatch 16 June 1991: 6B.

Karlsrud, Katherine. "Helping Dads Help Out." Parents' Magazine May
1990: 200.

Laskin, David. "Make Room For Daddy." Redbook Mar. 1990:
122-123 + 182-186.

Straus, Hal. "Freaks of Nurture." American Health Jan. - Feb. 1989:
70-71.

The following is a sample argumentative paper that was written for an **Essay and Research** class. This paper focuses on an issue of policy: Should American cities be required to institute mandatory recycling for household solid wastes?

As you read the paper, notice the Need-Plan-Practicality order. The student has used many of his own comments and explanations.

Remember, the pages have been boxed to simulate a page layout. Your pages should have at least a one-inch margin on all sides.

Mandatory Recycling:

The Solution for America's Trash Problem

by

Charles Scott Dembowski

for

Essay and Research

Mr. Martin

June 10, 19xx

Outline

Thesis statement: American cities should institute mandatory recycling for household solid wastes.

1. The sheer volume of solid waste is more than many communities can handle.

2. The wide range of materials also makes disposal difficult.

3. More dangerous than the solid waste is the amount of toxic waste in the landfills.

4. The cost for disposing of so much trash is enormous.

5. Since this solid waste problem is so complex, there are no simple answers for it.

6. While recycling is the best starting point for solving the solid waste problem, the success of the plan depends on how it is implemented.

7. Legislation is a method to promote, or mandate, recycling.

8. Educating the public and promoting the plan are the make-or-break elements for the program's success.

9. The degree of motivation people need often depends on their educational and socio-economic level.

10. Some towns make recycling a matter of personal as well as civic pride.

11. Of all the recycling methods available, the most successful but most costly service to run is curbside collection that utilizes a convenient method of in-house sorting.

12. At apartment complexes using dumpsters, large color-coded bins can be available to facilitate the recycling process for renters.

13. Although household recycling is the first step in a solution of the solid waste problem, it does have its critics.

14. Some people also complain that recycling solves too little of the trash problem to make a difference.

15. Besides being the first step in solving the solid waste crisis, recycling has many other benefits.

Conclusion: The solid waste problem has reached a state of chaos in America. Waste production is growing, and the landfills cannot accommodate it. Home recycling offers not only the best solution but also the benefits of new jobs, the preservation of the environment, and a new way of thinking about trash.

1

Mandatory Recycling:

The Solution for America's Trash Problem

Every day the average American produces three to five pounds of trash. When this amount is multiplied by the number of people in major cities such as New York (7,263,000), Los Angeles (2,967,000), or Philadelphia (1,700,000), one can see the enormity of the problem facing urban America. However, most cities are losing the battle against trash. In "Buried Alive," Melinda Beck reports that "more than two thirds of the nation's landfills have closed since the late 1970s [and] one third of those remaining will be full in the next five years" (67). And most communities are not willing to develop new landfills; they have developed a NIMBY syndrome (Not In My Backyard). Yet some cities have set a positive example by forcing residents to recycle. The successful programs ease the strain on landfills, create jobs, and help save natural resources. They are models to be emulated. In fact, American cities should institute mandatory recycling for household solid wastes.

Introduction establishes the problem, defines the issue, and builds credibility.

Thesis states the writer's opinion on the policy issue.

Dembowski 2

America is in the midst of a solid waste crisis. The extent of this crisis can be seen by considering how much refuse there is, what kinds create the problem, and how much it costs to get rid of it.

The sheer volume of solid waste is more than many communities can handle. A <u>Newsweek</u> cover story estimates that the volume of trash has increased 80 percent since 1960 and is predicted to grow an additional 20 percent by 2000 (Beck 67). Because 160 million tons of trash is hard to picture, Beck makes it more graphic by saying it is "enough to spread 30 stories high over 1,000 football fields, enough to fill a bumper-to-bumper convoy of garbage trucks halfway to the moon" (67).

The wide range of materials also makes disposal difficult. In <u>American City & County</u>, Bill Eldred gives the following breakdown: newspaper, cardboard, and mixed paper (27.5 percent), yard waste (17.9), glass (8.9), plastic (3.7), and steel or aluminum cans and containers (3.7) (58). Compounding the problem of volume is the fact that much of what is thrown away cannot or does not decompose. In a compost pile table scraps

Dembowski 2

such as banana or apple peels will rot into usable fertilizer. But in a landfill there is not enough sunlight or oxygen to promote the rotting. As a result, trash management experts maintain that hot dogs and corncobs remain recognizable and newspapers remain readable after more than 25 years in a landfill (Beck 70). Even diapers and trash bags designed to break down cannot do so because they fail to receive enough sunlight for photodecomposition.

More dangerous than the solid waste is the amount of toxic waste in the landfills. Although household chemicals, solvents, paint thinners, and used oil are supposed to be disposed of properly, they often end up in public landfills. Some current landfills have been described as toxic waste playgrounds. Stephen Budiansky and Robert Black in "Tons and Tons of Trash" found that the Fresh Kills Landfill at Staten Island leaks four million gallons of toxic waste a day into nearby streams which is almost 93 gallons a second. The Meadowlands landfill in New Jersey sits in over 40 feet of toxic waste (58). In other states similar landfills are leaking, contaminating ground water,

Part three of NEED: kinds of refuse-- liquids.

Dembowski 4

and creating a danger that may be greater than other forms of hazardous wastes.

Part four of NEED: the cost.

The cost for disposing of so much trash is enormous. In 1987, Eldred reported that the national average cost for dumping one ton of trash was $20 but that "environmental restrictions and scarce landfills have pushed disposal costs to more than $25 per ton in many cities and to as high as $125 per ton in parts of New York" (57). But before haulers can dump the trash, they must first get it to the landfill. Every year nearly 30,000 tons of trash are carried on the nation's highways. Some New England towns, according to Budiansky and Black, dispatch garbage trucks 24 hours a day to Ohio and other mid-western states (58). Beck reports that Long Island township alone spends approximately $23 million yearly to ship its trash out of state (67).

This section introduces the PLAN.

Since the solid waste problem is so complex, there are no simple answers for it. Most representatives from government and industry, along with waste management experts, agree that a solution will need at least three parts: recycling, burning, and

Dembowski 5

burying. In the broadest sense, recycling is the separation and reuse of materials to reduce the total amount of trash. What cannot be reused might then be burned to generate power and further break down the materials. The remaining ash that cannot be further processed is then buried in the landfill. While all parts of the solution are essential, it begins by requiring cities to institute mandatory recycling policies for homeowners.

While recycling is the best starting point in solving the solid waste problem, the success of the plan depends on how it is implemented. A high level of participation from the public means a convenient way to collect the materials must exist. In rural America, since a large number of people must haul their own trash to a dump anyway, a "drop-off" center for recyclables might be best suited for their community. Without the added cost of collection, recycling in this manner could be nothing but cost effective. Budiansky and Black point out that those living in the city are the major trash producers, generating over four pounds per person per day; requiring them to haul their refuse to a central collection site just would not work (31).

Imple-
mentation
of plan.

Dembowski 6

Imple-
mentation
through
legislation.

Legislation is a method to promote, or mandate, recycling. Without legislation, a recycling program must depend on volunteers. When this approach has been tried, a few people typically participate but not enough to make a significant difference. Through legislation the results are improved. So far, fourteen states have mandated recycling, and over 500 counties across the U.S. offer some form of curbside collections. According to Budiansky and Black, states such as Oregon and New Jersey estimate they recycle over 20% of their solid waste (30).

Imple-
mentation
through
legislation.

Educating the public and promoting the plan are the make-or-break elements for the program's success. In "Waste Disposal Issues Surveyed," Schwarz and Shelstad found that most experts agree on at least one thing: the key element is how the plan is presented to the public (44). When properly motivated, the public eagerly supports recycling. The effort seems to provide an outlet for their apprehensions about the environment. They cannot do anything about the depletion of the ozone or the greenhouse effect. But recycling gives them a concrete way to

Dembowski 7

show that they are doing their part.

The degree of motivation people need often depends on their educational and socio-economic level. Better educated and more affluent people generally support recycling programs. However, low-income families in America seem to need more motivation. Rather than develop penalties, program administrators have sought positive incentives. Goldoftas describes an imaginative system developed in the Bronx area of New York; there the local government uses a "buy-back" system, paying participators a certain amount of money for the products that they saved (33).

Some towns make recycling a matter of personal as well as civic pride. In "Recycling: Coming of Age," Barbara Goldoftas reviews the system used in Voorhees Township, Pennsylvania. Not only does that town urge everyone to participate but also places a stigma on those who do not. Each house is given a pail to be used for recyclable items, such as glass or aluminum. On trash pick-up day, the pail, used or not, must be placed outside along with other trash. If the pail is missing, a large red tag

Gaining public acceptance, adjusting to socio-economic level.

Gaining public acceptance-- example.

Dembowski 8

is placed on the trash, and the trash is left until the next collection day. Voorhees Township claims 100% success (32).

Of all the recycling methods available, the most successful, but most costly service to run is curbside collection utilizing a convenient method of in-house sorting. In this approach colored collection pails about the size of small waste baskets are issued for inside the home. Each color represents a recyclable article, such as glass, aluminum, or paper. For each pail inside the house, an outside, same-colored bin is set up to empty the smaller pails into. These bins, similar to a small outdoor trash can, are then placed at the curb for collection. When homeowners have a convenient way to sort the recyclables in the house, sorting costs at a processing plant are minimized.

At apartment complexes using dumpsters, large color-coded bins can be available to facilitate the recycling process for renters. Apartment managers must then educate and motivate tenants to separate their trash. So far, managers have used contests and appeals to community spirit to urge participation.

Example of a feasible program for homes.

A program for apartments.

Dembowski 9

Some have had to rely on spot checks of tenants' trash and to issue warnings or fines for violations.

Although household recycling is the first step in a solution of the solid waste problem, it does have its critics. First, many Americans clearly dislike the inconvenience of recycling their trash. According to U.S. News and World Report, these people think it is too inconvenient to remove lids from glass jars, wash them out, and keep them separate from the tin cans in the trash (Budiansky and Black 61). Yet this chore seems minor and not very time-consuming when one considers how much time people spend weekly on leisure and recreation activities. Surely, most people can spare a few minutes each day to recycle.

Acknowledges the opposition and refutes it.

Some people also complain that recycling solves too little of the trash problem to make a difference. It is true that recycling is not the entire solution. At best the most effective programs in America recycle about 25 to 50 percent of household trash; the rest is burned or buried in landfills. In Newsweek, Sharon Begley and Patricia King note that in Japan, which has a much better established recycling program than the U.S.,

Acknowledges the opposition and refutes it.

Dembowski 10

only about "40 percent of solid waste is recycled, including half the paper, about 55 percent of glass bottles and 66 percent of food and beverage cans" (76). Critics must realize the danger that can develop when no more landfills exist. A three-part plan--recycling, burning, and burying-- can extend the life of the nation's landfills until more effective ways of solving the problem can be found.

Outlines further benefits of the PLAN.

Besides being the first step in solving the solid waste crisis, recycling has many other benefits. Beck concludes that recycling "holds the edge in creating new jobs, protecting the environment, and conserving natural resources" (71). Investments abound for people with creative ideas for reprocessing trash or for making recycled goods competitive with those produced from virgin materials. Most important, citizen involvement in the solution may make them more aware of their role as contributors to the problem. If all Americans must sort and recycle their trash, they may abandon their throw-away mentality.

Dembowski 11

"We will need to have chaos in the area of solid waste before the problem is truly addressed," said David Sussman, vice president of environmental affairs with Ogden Martin Systems, Fairfield, N.J. (Treadaway 42). Unfortunately, this country has reached that point of chaos. The rate of waste production is growing and the landfills are full with little chance of more being developed. A solution must be found. As one element in a three-part plan, home recycling offers the best solution for this problem. Having been adopted by several states, recycling is poised for rapid growth, attracting hundreds of millions of dollars in investments, creating thousands of new jobs, and affording the potential for a new generation of environmentally sound packaging of consumer goods. While a period of adjustment may be necessary, recycling appears to be a permanent addition in the handling of solid waste.

Conclusion summarizes paper, reinforces thesis.

Dembowski 12

Works Cited

Beck, Melinda. "Buried Alive." <u>Newsweek</u> 27 Nov. 1989: 66-76.

Begley, Sharon, and Patricia King. "The Supply-Side Theory of
  Garbage." <u>Newsweek</u> 27 Nov. 1989: 76.

Budiansky, Stephen, and Robert Black. "Tons and Tons of Trash and
  No Place to Put it." <u>U.S. News and World Report</u> 14 Dec. 1987:
  58-62.

Eldred, Bill. "Changing Economics Revives Recycling. <u>American
  City and County</u> Dec. 1987: 57-69.

Goldoftas, Barbara. "Recycling: Cutting the Waste in Trash."
  <u>Technology Review</u> Nov./Dec. 1987: 28-35+.

Schwarz, Stephen, and Merlin J. Shelstad. "Waste Disposal Issues
  Surveyed." <u>American City and County</u> Feb. 1987: 42-53.

Treadaway, Dan. "Putting the Squeeze on America's Landfills."
  <u>American City and County</u> Aug. 1989: 42-50.

As a Columbus State student, you may find yourself in a literature class to fulfill a graduation requirement or to satisfy your own desire to read and discuss literature. Most of these literature courses require some writing. You have already seen how to construct a bibliography entry for your sources. But there are some special techniques for documenting these sources in your paper. On the following pages you can see how to document prose, poetry, and drama. After that you can see these techniques applied first to a journal entry for a short story and then to a paper that was written for a section of Introduction to Literature (1031).

DOCUMENTATION FORMAT FOR PROSE

1. Use MLA documentation form to reference quotations from a prose work. <u>Any</u> end punctuation is placed <u>outside</u> the page reference in parentheses (4 or fewer lines of text).

    "Then she would be married--she, Eveline. People would treat her

    with respect then" (4).

    "You see he does not believe I am sick! And what can one do" (88)?

    "Jim certainly was a card" (77)!

2. At the end of the journal entry or literary paper, the work(s) you are discussing should be presented in bibliographic form. Double-space the entry; the first line is at the left margin, and subsequent lines in the entry are indented 5 spaces. Names of short stories are enclosed in quotation marks. Include all pages on which the story appears.

    Joyce, James. "Eveline." <u>Literature and the Writing Process</u>. 2nd ed.

        Eds. Elizabeth McMahan, Susan Day, and Robert Funk. New

        York: Macmillan, 1989. 4-6.

3. A short quotation (4 lines or fewer as typed on <u>your</u> typewriter) is incorporated, double-spaced, into your text. A long quotation (more than 4 lines as typed on <u>your</u> typewriter) is indented 10 spaces from the left margin, double-spaced, and does not need to be enclosed in quotation marks. Documentation is <u>outside</u> the end punctuation. If the cited passage also starts a paragraph, indent it five spaces.

         It is a big airy room, the whole floor nearly, with

    windows that look all ways, and air and sunshine galore. It

    was nursery first and then playroom and gymnasium, I [the

    narrator] should judge; for the windows are barred for

little children, and there are rings and things in the

wall . . . I am sitting by the window . . . in this atrocious

nursery. (89)

**Note that the above quotation uses brackets: [   ]. Any comments or clarification that you insert into a quotation should be set off this way.

**Whenever you must omit any words from a quotation (to simplify or make the passage shorter) indicate the omitted words with an ellipsis: . . .

SAMPLES: USE OF QUOTATION MARKS IN PROSE DOCUMENTATION

FEWER THAN 4 LINES

1. **Narrative**

Original:

In ten years of walking by night or day, for thousands of miles, he had never met another person walking, not one in all that time.

How it will look in your paper:

"In ten years of walking by night or day, for thousands of miles, he had

never met another person walking, not one in all that time" (105).

2. **Dialogue (one speaker)**

Original:

"I guess you'd call me a writer."

How it will look in your paper:

"'I guess you'd call me a writer'" (105).

3. **Dialogue (more than one speaker, all dialogue occurring in the same paragraph)**

Original:

"I've been looking all over this hotel for you," said Mrs. Mitty. "Why do you have to hide in this old chair? How do you expect me to find you?" "Things close in," said Walter Mitty vaguely.

How it will look in your paper:

"'I've been looking all over this hotel for you,' said Mrs. Mitty. 'Why do

you have to hide in this old chair? How do you expect me to find you?'

'Things close in,' said Walter Mitty vaguely" (51).

MORE THAN 4 LINES

1. **Narrative**

<u>Original</u>:

Out of another I get a lovely view of the bay and a little private wharf belonging to the estate. There is a beautiful shaded lane that runs down there from the house. I always fancy I see people walking in these numerous paths and arbors, but John has cautioned me not to give way to fancy in the least.

<u>How it will look in your paper</u>:

Out of another [window] I get a lovely view of the bay

and a little private wharf belonging to the estate. There is

a beautiful shaded lane that runs down there from the

house. I always fancy I see people walking in these

numerous paths and arbors, but John has cautioned me not

to give way to fancy in the least. (90)

2. **Dialogue (one speaker)**

<u>Original</u>:

"And is it fitting," resumed the Reverend Mr. Clark, "that a man so given to prayer, of such a blameless example, holy in deed and thought, so far as mortal judgment may pronounce; is it fitting that a father in the church should leave a shadow on his memory, that may seem to blacken a life so pure?"

<u>How it will look in your paper</u>:

"And is it fitting," resumed the Reverend Mr. Clark,

"that a man so given to prayer, of such a blameless

example, holy in deed and thought, so far as mortal

judgment may pronounce; is it fitting that a father in the

church should leave a shadow on his memory, that may

seem to blacken a life so pure?" (117)

3.   Dialogue (more than one speaker)

<u>Original</u>:

"Just walking, Mr. Mead?"
"Yes."
"But you haven't explained for what purpose."
"I explained; for air and to see, and just to walk."
"Have you done this often?"
"Every night for years."

<u>How it will look in your paper</u>:

"Just walking, Mr. Mead?"

"Yes."

"But you haven't explained for what purpose."

"I explained; for air and to see, and just to walk."

"Have you done this often?"

"Every night for years." (106)

In examples 2 and 3 above, the long quotation is enclosed in quotation
marks because it begins and ends with dialogue. In the following example,
quotations are used only for the internal dialogue.

<u>Original</u>:

Mr. Graves took the hand of the little boy, who came willingly with him up to
the box. "Take a paper out of the box, Davy," Mr. Summers said. Davy put
his hand into the box and laughed. "Take just one paper," Mr. Summers
said. "Harry, you hold it for him." Mr. Graves took the child's hand and
removed the folded paper from the tight fist and held it while little Dave
stood next to him and looked up at him wonderingly.

How it will look in your paper:

Mr. Graves took the hand of the little boy, who came willingly with him up to the box. "Take a paper out of the box, Davy," Mr. Summers said. Davy put his hand into the box and laughed. "Take just one paper," Mr. Summers said. "Harry, you hold it for him." Mr. Graves took the child's hand and removed the folded paper from the tight fist and held it while little Dave stood next to him and looked up at him wonderingly. (61)

DOCUMENTATION FORMAT FOR POETRY

1.   In your introduction, use the MLA style to document the sentence that mentions the title of the poem and the author.

   Stephen Spender uses powerful imagery to create a picture of the inner city in his poem "An Elementary School Classroom in a Slum" (588-9).

   Metaphor is the main figure of speech used in Randall Jarrell's "The Death of the Ball Turret Gunner" (593).

2.   At the end of the entry or literary paper, include a bibliography entry to identify the poem and source. Titles of poems are enclosed within quotation marks.

   Spender, Stephen. "An Elementary School Classroom in a Slum." <u>Literature and the Writing Process</u>. 2nd end. Eds. Elizabeth McMahan, Susan Day, and Robert Funk. New York: Macmillan, 1989. 588-9.

3.   If you are quoting 3 or fewer lines of poetry, incorporate the lines into your text. However, you must indicate the end of each line with a slash. Document by using line numbers:

<u>Original</u>:

Had we but world enough, and time,
This coyness, lady, were no crime.

<u>Sample passage from journal entry or paper</u>:

In "To His Coy Mistress" by Andrew Marvell, the <u>carpe</u>

<u>diem</u> theme is stressed: "Had we but world enough, and

time,/This coyness, lady, were no crime" (ll. 1-2).

Notice that you **must** include the original punctuation of the poem.

4. You <u>must</u> use an ellipsis to indicate omitted words and brackets to indicate words you insert for clarification.

    If you are quoting only one line of poetry, use one "l." (l. 3)

5. For quotations longer than 3 lines of poetry, double-space and set off the quotation by indenting 10 spaces from the left margin. Use the same line arrangement you see in the original. If a line is too long, continue it on the next line but indent it as shown here.

            I am the poet of the Body and I am the poet of

                the Soul,

            The pleasures of heaven are with me the pains

                of hell are with me,

            The first I graft and increase upon myself,

the latter I translate into a new tongue.

I am the poet of the woman the same as the

man,

And I say it is as great to be a woman as to

be a man.

And I say there is nothing greater than the

mother of men.   (ll. 422-27)

DOCUMENTATION FORMAT FOR DRAMA

When documenting drama, distinguish between plays that are written in prose and those that are written in poetry. Also distinguish between plays divided into acts and scenes and those which are not.

1.   In your introduction, use the MLA style for the sentence that mentions the title of the play and the author.

> Arthur Miller paints a grim picture of the American Dream in
>
> Death of a Salesman (931-991).

2.   Include a bibliography citation at the end of the journal entry or literary paper. Underline titles of plays.

> Miller, Arthur. Death of a Salesman. Literature and the Writing
>
> Process. 2nd ed. Eds. Elizabeth McMahan, Susan Day, and
>
> Robert Funk. New York: Macmillan, 1989. 931-991.

3.   For a play written in prose, such as Death of a Salesman, document citations by using the same style described for fiction.

> Willy idolizes his son Biff: ". . . you got a greatness in you, Biff,
>
> remember that. You got all kinds a greatness . . ." (958).

4.   For more than 4 lines of quotation, indent 10 spaces from the left margin, double-space, and do not enclose the passage within quotation marks.

> WILLY.   I'm fat. I'm very---foolish to look at,
>
> Linda. I didn't tell you, but Christmas time I
>
> happened to be calling on F. H. Stewarts, and a
>
> salesman I know, as I was going in to see the
>
> buyer, I heard him say something about--
>
> walrus. . . . I won't take that. (944)

5.   For plays whose lines are written as poetry, use line documentation. If the play is divided into parts such as prologue, acts, scenes, epilogue, you will need to indicate the sections in your documentation. Use Arabic numerals separated by periods for acts and/or scenes. Do not use "l" or "ll" for line or lines. Notice that in short citations the final punctuation comes <u>after</u> the parenthetical reference; in long citations it comes <u>before</u> the parenthetical reference.

1 - 3 LINES

Antigone is prepared to die: "Surely this is no hardship:

can anyone / Living, as I live, with evil all about me, / Think

Death less than a Friend" (2.67-69)?

Antigone has no fear of Creon: "Creon is not strong

enough to stand in my way" (Pro. 35).

MORE THAN 3 LINES

> BRABANTIO.   A maiden never bold;
>
> Of spirit so still and quiet, that her motion
>
> Blush'd at herself; and she, in spite of
>
> nature,
>
> Of years, of country, credit, every thing,
>
> To fall in love with what she fear'd to look
>
> on! (1.3.95-99)

SAMPLE JOURNAL ENTRY

Jana Thompson

Miss Principe

Intro to Lit--1031

25 Oct. 19xx

Psyching Out One's Opponent

Introduction names author and title.

It is said that every man has his price, a weakness that "The others may use to manipulate him. In Edgar Allan Poe's Cask of Amontillado," the narrator exploits the

States thesis.

weakness of his antagonist in order to gain revenge (119-123).

Montresor, the narrator of Poe's tale, has apparently been perpetually annoyed with Fortunato until he reaches

Quotations use MLA documentation.

his breaking point, whereupon Montresor exclaims, ". . . but when he ventured upon insult, I vowed revenge" (119). Montresor determines to avenge himself and determines he must do so without being found out: "I must not only

Short quotations in the text.

punish but punish with impunity" (119). He decides to take advantage by capitalizing on Fortunato's Achilles' heel: "He had a weak point . . . . He prided himself on his connoisseurship of wine" (119). Montresor is also

Thompson 2

a connoisseur and decides to use his knowledge of
wines to entrap Fortunato.

Montresor's clever exploitation of Fortunato's
weakness is evident in the following exchange:

> ". . . I have received . . . what passes for
> Amontillado, and I have my doubts I
> was silly enough to pay the full
> Amontillado price without consulting you
> in the matter."
>
> "Amontillado!"
>
> "I have my doubts."
>
> "Amontillado!"
>
> "And I must satisfy them."
>
> "Amontillado!"
>
> "As you are engaged, I am on my way
> to Luchesi . . . . He will tell me--"
>
> "Luchesi cannot tell Amontillado
> from Sherry . . . . Come, let us go."
>
> "Whither?"
>
> "To your vaults." (119-120)

Long quotations blocked.

Ellipses indicate material has been omitted.

Thompson 3

Montresor cleverly uses reverse psychology to
entrap Fortunato. The more he protests that Fortunato
not accompany him, the more Fortunato is intrigued.
Ironically, it is Fortunato who suggests they go to
Montresor's vault. Montresor has also practiced reverse
psychology on his servants and has exploited
their weakness:

> I had told them that I should not return until
> the morning, and had given them explicit
> orders not to stir from the house. These
> orders were sufficient, I well knew, to insure
> their immediate disappearance, one and all,
> as soon as my back was turned. (120)

As Montresor and Fortunato travel through the vault,
Fortunato begins to cough from the dampness. Montresor
repeatedly attempts to dissuade his friend from continuing,
of course with the opposite result, which is exactly how
Montresor has planned it. Finally Montresor lures
Fortunato into a dead end and proceeds to wall up the niche,
burying Fortunato alive! Every man has his price, and in
this instance, the price is too high; Fortunato pays with his
life.

Long quotation blocked and double-spaced.

Thompson 4

Work Cited

Poe, Edgar Allan. "The Cask of Amontillado." <u>Literature</u>
<u>and the Writing Process</u>. 2nd ed. Eds. Elizabeth
McMahan, Susan Day, and Robert Funk. New York:
Macmillan, 1989. 119-123.

Bibliography
entry to
reference story
and source.

Richard Bratt
Intro to Lit 1031
Mrs. Thompson
Winter 1990

Out of Control

The inability to change one's situation is a common theme in literature. Ray Bradbury is a modern writer who has used this theme, and Sophocles is a classical Greek tragedian who was a master at portraying human foibles. A comparison of Bradbury's "The Pedestrian" and Sophocles' Antigone will clearly show that both writers have used an individual's inability to control his or her world as a central theme for their works.

In "The Pedestrian," the main character, Leonard Mead, does not conform to the society he is a part of. Unfortunately, Leonard is one man against millions and hence has no control in his own world. Leonard is a dreamer, an anachronism in a world that has lost its spark for life. The citizens of this world of 2053 A.D. have begun to isolate themselves from other citizens. Leonard has the unheard of habit of taking nightly walks and has never encountered another person in all that time:

Bratt 2

. . . on his way he would see the cottages and homes
with their dark windows, and it was not unequal to
walking through a graveyard . . . . Sudden gray
phantoms seemed to manifest upon inner room walls
. . . or there were whisperings and murmurs where a
window in a tomblike building was still open. (104)

Leonard's society is one that, in effect, rolls up the
sidewalks at sunset; the people of this world simply do not leave
their houses after dark. At nightfall, the inhabitants of this
futuristic society retreat to their homes/caves and huddle
around their viewing screens/fires. Leonard, however, likes to
venture outdoors in the evening, but the people of this society
have developed ways of dealing with people like Leonard. In a
wonderfully ironic passage, Bradbury describes Leonard's
encounter with the "police":

A metallic voice called to him:

"Stand still. Stay where you are! Don't move!"

He halted.

"Put up your hands!"

"But---" he said.

"Your hands up! Or we'll shoot!"

The police, of course, but what a rare incredible

thing; in a city of three million, there was only one

police car left . . . . (105)

Leonard is subjected to intense questioning; the "police"

cannot believe he is just out for a walk. When queried why,

Leonard replies, "I explained; for air, and to see, and just to walk

. . . " (106). The "police" can't imagine why he isn't home like

everyone else, glued to the viewing screen. Two final ironies are

revealed: the "police" are really an automated police car with no

one in it, and at the conclusion of the story, Leonard is on his

way to the "Psychiatric Center for Research on Regressive

Tendencies" (106). It certainly would not do to have a nature

walker in a society that travels everywhere by car and huddles at

home around the television at night.

Leonard Mead's society will not tolerate people who do not

conform to its standards. Leonard's behavior is considered

eccentric and dangerous, so he is whisked off to an asylum

simply because he will not conform. He has tried to rebel and exert some measure of control in his world and has failed. There is simply nothing he can do to change his situation, for he is one against many. Clearly, Leonard a person who has no control of the world around him.

"The Pedestrian" presents the reader with a man who finds himself in an alien and hostile futuristic world, while <u>Antigone</u> reveals a woman who is trapped in an ancient world dominated by men. Yet despite the difference in eras and sexes, there is not much difference between the situations in which the two protagonists find themselves.

<u>Antigone</u> tells the story of the cursed remaining members of the family of Oedipus. His two sons, Eteocles and Polyneices, have died in a battle to decide the kingship of Thebes after Oedipus' death. Since Polyneices led the attack on Thebes, Creon, the new king, has declared that Polyneices be left unburied, while Eteocles be interred with full military honors. Antigone, the sister of Eteocles and Polyneices, desires to follow the divine law that states all should be given a proper burial.

This is the central conflict between Antigone and her antagonist Creon.

Antigone is discovered in her attempt to bury Polyneices and is brought before Creon. She pleads her case well, but because she is a mere woman, Creon will not listen. He is jealous of his new kingship and will not tolerate anyone, especially a woman, challenging his authority.

> Creon. . . . Had you heard my proclamation
> touching this matter?
> Antigone. It was public. Could I help hearing it?
> Creon. And yet you dared defy the law?
> Antigone.   I dared.
> It was not God's proclamation. . . .
> Your edict, King, was strong,
> But all your strength is weakness itself against
> The immortal unrecorded laws of God. (2.54-61)

In this ancient world, it is unheard of for a woman to stand against any man, let alone the king. Creon will not even consider listening to the arguments of a woman. Therefore,

Antigone has no control over the treatment of her brother's remains, and, in larger way, over her world in general.

Later in the play, Creon is confronted with both women, Antigone and her sister Ismene, and accuses both of treason. His attitude toward women is very clear when he exclaims to the Chorus: "Gentlemen, I beg you to observe these girls:/One has just now lost her mind; the other,/It seems, has never had a mind at all" (2.150-152). It is clear that women in ancient Greece possessed no political power; nor were they considered men's equals. Therefore, they have no control over the vast majority of events in their world. The reader knows that Antigone, like Leonard, is doing the "right thing." Yet her world is as hostile about her burying Polyneices as Mead's world is about his walking at night.

"The Pedestrian" and <u>Antigone</u> both present the reader with protagonists who have no control over their worlds. Leonard is an outcast, an eccentric, and his opinions and feelings are considered regressive by a society who, ironically, is more regressive than he is. Antigone is a woman whose only desire is to follow her religious and moral convictions by giving her brother a decent burial; however, as a woman of ancient Greece, she has slightly more freedom than a slave.

Finally, both stories deal with a loss of humanity and compassion. Leonard Mead's society will not tolerate those who are "different," and the officials will program those with divergent thoughts so that they will become as dehumanized as the rest of the society. In Antigone's society, its ruler has lost all compassion. He does not see a courageous woman who wants to adhere to divine law, but sees a woman who attempts to usurp his power. Both protagonists meet their ultimate fate at the hands of these cruel societies---Antigone commits suicide after being buried alive, and Leonard will be programmed to sit in front of a "viewing screen" like the rest of his dead society.

Bratt 8

Works Cited

Bradbury, Ray. "The Pedestrian." <u>Literature and the Writing Process</u>. 2nd ed. Eds. Elizabeth McMahan, Susan Day, and Robert Funk. New York: Macmillan, 1989. 104-106.

Sophocles. <u>Antigone</u>. <u>Literature and the Writing Process</u>. 2nd ed. Eds. Elizabeth McMahan, Susan Day, and Robert Funk. New York: Macmillan, 1989. 632-656.

Selected Revision Checklist

Your answers to these questions should be "yes." If the answer to a question is "no," revision is needed.

1. Does your paper have a prefatory outline?

2. Is there a separate introductory paragraph? Does it attract your readers' attention, focus the topic, establish credibility with source material, and lead to the thesis?

3. Does your thesis name your specific topic, provide an attitude, judgment, or direction that the rest of the paper will develop? See relevant pages to distinguish between expository and argumentative thesis statements.

4. Does each supporting section have a clear topic sentence? Is there sentence variety?

5. Have you avoided the use of borrowed material in your topic sentences? It is all right for introductory or concluding paragraphs. Otherwise, use topic sentences for developmental paragraphs.

6. Do you have at least one body paragraph for each of your main points?

7. Can the material in each body paragraph be effectively managed in a single paragraph?

8. Do you have a lead-in for all borrowed material, whether quoted, summarized, or paraphrased?

9. Have you used a variety of lead-in devices? Complete or generic lead-ins for first time use and shorter forms for subsequent uses of a source?

10. Is there variety in your lead-in language? Grammatical soundness?

    Avoid: In Bill Smith's article ". . . ," he says . . . .

11. Have you put long quotations (4 typed lines) in block form with no quotation marks? Have you introduced block quotations with a complete sentence followed by a colon?

12. Have you avoided needless quoting of sources and opted instead for summaries and paraphrases?

13. Have you included your own reactions, attitudes, and information into the research paper?

14. Does your conclusion develop logically out of the body rather than seeming to be tacked on?

15. Does your conclusion avoid a repetitive-sounding summary but still leave your reader with something relevant and important? Consider looking to the future, stressing the importance of the topic. Do not introduce new points of development!

16. Does your paper stay within the required page length?

17. Further revision suggested by your instructor:

Selected Editing Concerns

1. Is your punctuation correct for quotations?

   a. When the quotation is introduced with a lead-in device, follow the lead-in with a comma.

      President Bush says, "My nomination to the Supreme Court will . . . ."

   b. When the quotation is introduced with "that," do not use a comma.

      President Bush says that his "nomination to the Supreme Court will . . . ."

   c. A block quotation should be introduced by a complete sentence followed by a colon.

      Some critics' warnings about the effects of electromagnetic fields are ominous:

   d. Put quotation marks around the titles of magazine and newspaper articles, chapter titles, and episodes of television programs.

2. Is your capitalization correct?

   a. Capitalize the first word of a quotation if it is formally introduced, as in 1a and 1c above.

   b. Do not capitalize the first word of a quotation if you have assimilated the quotation into your own sentence structure (with "that"). See 1b above.

   c. Capitalize the first word of a quotation of a title or subtitle and all significant words in the title.

      Non-significant words are the following: **a, an, the** conjunctions and prepositions of fewer than four letters: **and, or, for, to, in,** etc.

3. Does the format of your paper follow that of the paper on bed and breakfasts?

4. Have you eliminated all major grammar and mechanical errors? No sentence fragments, run-on sentences (fused sentences), subject-verb disagreements, verb-form errors. Comma splice errors and spelling errors are also high-priority editing concerns.

5. Have you eliminated all contractions? For instance, change <u>don't</u>, <u>won't</u>, and <u>can't</u> to <u>do not</u>, <u>will not</u>, and <u>cannot</u>.

6. Have you avoided sexist language? Avoid sexist job titles such as chairwoman, policeman, and salesman. Prefer neutral terms such as chairperson, police officer, and sales representative.

   Avoid awkward pronoun reference such as:

An individual	They
A child	He or she
A nurse	Him or her

   Instead prefer plural nouns:

People	They, their, them
Children	They, their, them
Nurses	They, their, them

7. Further editing concerns:

Editing Checklist

1.   Are all sentences complete?
   frag--The newest member of the Supreme Court.

2.   Have you avoided run-on sentences--two sentences run together without punctuation between them?
   fs--Working long hours at a computer may be dangerous it might trigger miscarriages.

3.   Have you avoided comma splices--two sentences incorrectly joined with a comma?
   cs--Working long hours at a computer may be dangerous, it might trigger miscarriages.

4.   Do all subjects agree with their verbs?
   SV agr--The Chief Justice and the other members of the Supreme Court wants to reconsider this issue. [The verb should be plural "want."]

5.   Are the verbs in the correct form?
   v--We were suppose to finish the paper by Thursday.
   [The verb should be "were supposed."]

6.   Is tense appropriate and consistent?
   t--The robber entered the room and looked around.
   He listens carefully to make sure no one is moving around the house. [The writer has switched to present tense in the second sentence.]

7.   Are all words spelled correctly?
   sp--

8.   Have you avoided word choice errors? Check dictionary for meanings and connotations.

9.   Do all pronouns have clear antecedents?
   ref--His father told him that he had to go shopping.
   [Who had to go shopping?]

10.   Do all pronouns and their antecedents agree?
   agr (PA)--A successful writer takes his time to work with several drafts. They also carefully proofread their final draft. [The plural pronouns "they" and "their" should not be used to refer to the singular noun "writer."]

Exercise: **Name:**_____

Defining College Research   **Meeting Days/Time:**_____

DIRECTIONS: The purpose of this exercise is for you to clarify for yourself what is meant by doing research in college writing. First read pages 1-5 of this guide. Then as directed by your instructor, plan written or oral responses to the following discussion questions.

Suppose you are writing on one of the following assigned topics:

buying a used car	applying for financial aid
coping with stress	finding a day care center
serving in the military	avoiding credit problems

1. How would your treatment of the topic differ if you write a research paper rather than a report or essay?

2. How could you incorporate your own experience into a research paper on this topic? Give an example.

3. List at least 5 different sources of information that would be available on this topic.

4. When you research to satisfy your need to know you usually limit your topic to 4 or 5 specific questions you want to answer. What 4 or 5 questions would you like to answer about this topic?

5. Compare your answers above with the summary definition of the research paper on page 5. Would your approach make a good start for a research paper?

Exercise: **Name:**_____

Selecting a Topic   **Meeting Days/Time:**_____

DIRECTIONS: The purpose of this section is to help you select workable topics for your research papers. Your research will be more successful if you have a strong interest in your topic and a great desire to learn. Because choosing a good topic is difficult, the following are being suggested. Most are broad and need further restriction. Many can be used for expository or argumentative papers. All can be adapted to suit your own interests.

Job related stress

Information related stress

Causes of Acid Rain

Oil and the environment

Factors contributing to birth defects

What is Epilepsy?

Alcoholism

Animal Rights

Drinking During Pregnancy

Breast-fed or Bottle Baby

Surrogate Motherhood

Ohio's New Domestic Violence Laws

The National Decline in Literacy

The WIC Program

Contraceptives

Recycling

Reform and Congress

Sex Education and the Public Schools

Midlife Crisis

Exercise and the Elderly

Effects of Caffeine

Statehood for Puerto Rico

Release of Mental Patients in the U.S.

Selecting a PC for Home (Office) Use

Alternative Energy Sources

Controlling Fear

Dress for Success

School related stress

Child Pornography

Clear--cutting

Heart attack

Runaway children

Dyslexia and You

Teenage Alcoholism

Prescription Drug Abuse

Effects of Eating Junk Food

Hunger in America

Wife Abuse

I.Q. Testing

Smoking and You

Crib Death

Finding a Balanced Vegetarian Diet

Abuse of the Elderly

The Truth about Jogging

Hyperactivity

Nutrition and the Elderly

DNA Experiments

New Laws to Ban Imports

Reincarnation

Office Automation

Nuclear Energy

Anger and Its Effects

Habitat for the Homeless

The Effects of Video Display Terminals

Self-Defense for Women
Effects of Laughter
Teach for America or other Peace Corps jobs
Children's Rights
Religious Cults
Euthanasia/Physician Assisted Suicide
Women and Combat
The Olympics and Politics
Earthquakes (or other natural disasters)
Workfare
Job Opportunities in (x) Field
Police Abuse
Assertiveness
Self-Esteem
Vital Factors in Maintaining Good Health
"Mainstreaming" and the Public Schools
The Government and the Tobacco Farmer
So When Am I An Adult?
Workers Comp and You
Competency Testing for (name occupation)
Social Security and You
Palestine and Israel
The Gulf Crisis
Water Conservation/Quality
Broadcasters' Equal-time Rule
Rape
Bungee Jumping
Invest in (name category)
Violence in Movies (or other media)
Open Adoption Records
Gun Control
Free Education?
Teens in Penal Institutions
Freedom Fighter or Terrorist?
Problems in the Inner Cities
NASA and Its Problems
Investigative Reporting
Hitler and the Jews
Adjustment to Retirement
The Importance of Fairy Tales
Same Sex Marriage/Parenting
The Art of Negotiation
Gardening

Art Censorship
Food for Peace
Treatment for Arthritis
Lifestyles of the Amish (or other group)
Computer Banking
Neutering Animals
A National Health
The High Cost of Dying
Congressional Perks
Hospital or Home Births
Females and Religious Persecution
Motivational Techniques in Management
Evolution of Rock Music
Increasing Self-esteem
Evolution of Jazz
Handicapped in America
Adoption Laws
Crazy Laws Still on the Books
Personal Injury and You
Competency testing to Graduate
Congress and a Balanced Budget
Rise of Neo Nazis
Food Labels
Inflation and You
Ohio's Seat Belt Law
Training Wages
Smoking
Peacetime Military Registration
Weather Forecasting
Slaughter of Fur Seals
Management of Wilderness Areas
Cutting Social Security Benefits
The Benefits of Swimming (or other sport)
Technology and Progress
EMTs
Developing Antarctica
The Role of Prejudice in our Lives
Gay and Lesbian Rights
Meditation
The Relationship of Humans with Animals
Sleep Disorders/Pills
A Home for the Palestinians
Zoos (or other animal preserves) and Their
    Importance

Exercise: **Name:**_____

Finding Material   **Meeting Days/Time:**_____

DIRECTIONS: To complete this exercise, first read pages 6-31 of this text. Then use one of the topics suggested on pages 248-249 or select one of your own. Then as directed by your instructor, prepare written or oral responses to the following discussion questions.

1.   Topic:

2.   How can you narrow the topic?

3.   What major terms would you need to define to explain this topic for someone?

4.   What dictionaries would be helpful in researching this topic?

5.   What general or specialized encyclopedias would be helpful in researching this topic?

6. How can you discover what books are available on this topic?

7. What periodicals would be helpful in researching this topic?

8. Which indexes would you use to locate articles in the periodicals named in #7?

9. What kinds of statistics could be helpful in developing this topic? Which sources could you use?

10. What nonprint sources might be helpful to gain information on this topic? (films, videos, records, documentaries?)

11. From your answers to the above questions, how workable do you consider the topic?

Exercise: Name:_____

Announcing Your Topic   Meeting Days/Time:_____

DIRECTIONS: Follow your instructor's guidelines for choosing a topic that can be developed into a research paper of four to six pages.

Use the space provided to brainstorm your answers. Then write a short essay of 200-300 words in which you explain why you have chosen to do your research on this topic. Justify your selection by answering the following questions.

1.   How have you narrowed the topic to the specific length of the assigned paper? What is the specific topic?

2.   Describe your personal motives for researching this topic.
      A.   Why are you personally interested in the topic?
      B.   What do you already know about the topic?
      C.   What do you want to learn about the topic?

3.   Is there a wide range of available material? Is the material recent enough to show that the topic is still current?

4.   How can the topic be developed into a paper of exposition? How can it be developed into an argument?

5.   Why is the topic important enough to warrant a research paper on it?

Exercise: Name:_____

Understanding Plagiarism Meeting Days/Time:_____

DIRECTIONS: THIS QUIZ is designed to test your understanding of the problem with plagiarism. Read pages 32-34 of this text. Indicate your responses to the following questions. Be ready to discuss your answers.

True	False		
_____	_____	1.	Plagiarism occurs only when you buy an essay and submit it as your own.
_____	_____	2.	More than 50% of college students admit to having plagiarized some assignments. Therefore, plagiarism must be an acceptable practice.
_____	_____	3.	There can be severe penalties for plagiarism.
_____	_____	4.	Acts of plagiarism are punished only in college.
_____	_____	5.	No one is hurt when plagiarism occurs.
_____	_____	6.	When students have used only the ideas contained in an article but no direct quotations, they do not need to document or give credit.

Exercise: Set I   **N a m e :**_____

Magazine Review   **Meeting Days/Time:**_____

DIRECTIONS: The purpose of this exercise is to introduce you to the periodical collection in the college library. By reviewing the magazines you can also discover workable topics for a research paper. As directed by your instructor, review at least two different copies of each magazine and complete this form with the required information.

1.   Name of Periodical: _____

      Corporate Publisher: _____

2.   How often is it published? _____

3.   Does the periodical have **continuous pagination** or does

      each issue start with page 1? _____

4.   Who is the **intended audience** of the magazine: students, professionals, teachers, the general public? How can you tell? Consider name, table of contents, language, visual aids, or advertisements.

5.   What are the typical **credentials** of the authors? Consider degrees, places of employment. Is the information provided? Look at the start or end of the article or for a section called "About our Contributors." If the credentials are not given or if the writers are all staff members, simply write "Credentials not immediately available."

6.   From the table of contents list four titles of main or **feature articles**. Select those titles that sound most interesting to you.

Issue I.   Date _____

Titles:

1.   _____

2.   _____

3.   _____

4.   _____

Issue II.   Date _____

Titles:

1.   _____

2.   _____

3.   _____

4.   _____

Possible topic: _____

      From this first review of magazines you may discover a topic that appeals to you for your research paper.

      When looking for topics, consider your technology or intended major as a field of employment or its job opportunities. Or your might investigate a particular trend, issue, controversy, problem, new products, services, regulations, etc.

      Your first choice of periodicals, may yield no results--topics that are too technical or uninteresting. In that case, consider other periodicals. Or look for workable topics from lecture notes, textbooks, or discussions with other students or with your instructor.

Exercise: Set II Name:_____

Magazine Review Meeting Days/Time:_____

DIRECTIONS: The purpose of this exercise is to introduce you to the periodical collection in the college library. By reviewing the magazines you can also discover workable topics for a research paper. As directed by your instructor, review at least two different copies of each magazine and complete this form with the required information.

1. Name of Periodical: _____

    Corporate Publisher: _____

2. How often is it published? _____

3. Does the periodical have **continuous pagination** or does

    each issue start with page 1? _____

4. Who is the **intended audience** of the magazine: students, professionals, teachers, the general public? How can you tell? Consider name, table of contents, language, visual aids, or advertisements.

5. What are the typical **credentials** of the authors? Consider degrees, places of employment. Is the information provided? Look at the start or end of the article or for a section called "About our Contributors." If the credentials are not given or if the writers are all staff members, simply write "Credentials not immediately available."

6. From the table of contents list four titles of main or **feature articles**. Select those titles that sound most interesting to you.

Issue I. **Date** _____

Titles:

1. _____

2. _____

3. _____

4. _____

Issue II. **Date** _____

Titles:

1. _____

2. _____

3. _____

4. _____

Possible topic: _____

From this first review of magazines you may discover a topic that appeals to you for your research paper.

When looking for topics, consider your technology or intended major as a field of employment or its job opportunities. Or your might investigate a particular trend, issue, controversy, problem, new products, services, regulations, etc.

Your first choice of periodicals, may yield no results--topics that are too technical or uninteresting. In that case, consider other periodicals. Or look for workable topics from lecture notes, textbooks, or discussions with other students or with your instructor.

Exercise: Set III   **N a m e:**_____

Magazine Review   **Meeting Days/Time:**_____

DIRECTIONS: The purpose of this exercise is to introduce you to the periodical collection in the college library. By reviewing the magazines you can also discover workable topics for a research paper. As directed by your instructor, review at least two different copies of each magazine and complete this form with the required information.

1.   Name of Periodical: _____

       Corporate Publisher: _____

2.   How often is it published? _____

3.   Does the periodical have **continuous pagination** or does

       each issue start with page 1? _____

4.   Who is the **intended audience** of the magazine: students, professionals, teachers, the general public? How can you tell? Consider name, table of contents, language, visual aids, or advertisements.

5.   What are the typical **credentials** of the authors? Consider degrees, places of employment. Is the information provided? Look at the start or end of the article or for a section called "About our Contributors." If the credentials are not given or if the writers are all staff members, simply write "Credentials not immediately available."

6. From the table of contents list four titles of main or **feature articles**. Select those titles that sound most interesting to you.

Issue I.   Date _____
Titles:

1. _____

2. _____

3. _____

4. _____

Issue II.   Date _____
Titles:

1. _____

2. _____

3. _____

4. _____

Possible topic: _____

From this first review of magazines you may discover a topic that appeals to you for your research paper.

When looking for topics, consider your technology or intended major as a field of employment or its job opportunities. Or your might investigate a particular trend, issue, controversy, problem, new products, services, regulations, etc.

Your first choice of periodicals, may yield no results--topics that are too technical or uninteresting. In that case, consider other periodicals. Or look for workable topics from lecture notes, textbooks, or discussions with other students or with your instructor.

Worksheet: **Name:** _____

Search Strategy   **Meeting Days/Time:** _____

DIRECTIONS: As directed by your instructor, complete the basic steps of the Search Strategy. Complete this form with the required information.

1. **YOUR TECHNOLOGY/MAJOR:** _____

  TENTATIVE TOPIC: _____

  SEARCH INTENDED FOR: Expository Essay _____

          Argumentative Essay ____

2. **SUBJECT HEADINGS:** (from Library of Congress Subject Headings, Cross Reference Index, or other sources)

  _____

  _____

  _____

3. **DICTIONARIES RELEVANT TO YOUR RESEARCH:**

  _____

  _____

  _____

4. **GENERAL OR SPECIALIZED ENCYCLOPEDIAS RELEVANT TO YOUR RESEARCH:**

  _____

  _____

  _____

5. **ONLINE CATALOG:** Are sources listed? What Dewey Decimal Numbers indicate where in the stacks the materials are?
    Dewey:_____

    _____

    _____

6. **PERIODICAL INDEXES/COMPUTER INDEXES:**

    _____

    _____

    _____

7. **JOURNALS IN THE FIELD TO CHECK ON:**

    _____

    _____

8. **OTHER PERIODICALS WHICH MAY BE HELPFUL:**

    _____

    _____

    _____

9. **OTHER SOURCES TO EXPLORE:** (consider experts in the field, instructors, textbooks, audio-visual media, site visits, etc.).

    _____

    _____

Exercise: **Level I**   **Name:**   _____

Paraphrasing   **Due:**   _____

Rephrase the following short passages using **your own words and sentence structures**.

A.   Chollar, Susan. "Food For Thought." Psychology Today Apr. 1988:

       30-34.

Rather than energizing, carbohydrates calm or even fatigue people and can decrease alertness and slow reaction time. For most, these symptoms are mild and brought on only by unbalanced-carbohydrate meals: meals with excessive amounts of sugars and starches but without protein such as cheese, meat, or eggs. (Chollar 30)

B.   Miller, Henry I., and Stephen J. Ackerman. "Perspective on Food

       Biotechnology." FDA Consumer 10 Mar. 1990: 8-13.

Unlike their predecessors, who progressed by trial and error, today's farmers can exploit the subtleties of genetics. Science has found ways for them to introduce quickly and directly specific crop and animal improvements that formerly took generations. The result may be the same, but the new precision multiplies the possibilities available for achieving specific practical results. (Miller and Ackerman 10)

C.   Pittman, Frank. "Betraying Trust: Modern-day Myths of Infidelity."

      Utne Reader Nov./Dec. 1991: 105-11.

     [It is a myth that] everyone has affairs. The data on the frequency of infidelity is fairly consistent. About half do and half don't. Traditionally, more men than women have been adulterous, but the women seem to be catching up. Surveys in the last few years tell us that about 50 percent of husbands have been unfaithful, while 30-40 percent of wives have been.

     If infidelity of some sort takes place in over half of all marriages, that's a lot of infidelity. The figures are misleading, though. Many adulterers have had only one affair, most only a few. Much of the infidelity takes place (as cause of effect) in the last year of a dying marriage. Intact, continuing marriages are far less adulterous. Marital fidelity remains the norm, since most marital partners are faithful most of the time. The same surveys that show most marriages as adulterous also show that the vast majority of people believe strongly in marital fidelity, certainly for their spouse and generally for themselves. It remains the ideal, even if it is not always achieved.

D.   Miller, George A. "The Challenge of Universal Literacy." Science 241

      (1988): 1293-99.

     Semiliteracy is a way of life for millions of U.S. citizens--estimates of how many vary depending on the definition of literacy that is used, but the number of these individuals living in poor urban neighborhoods has increased rapidly since 1970. Many of them are unable to follow written instructions, pass a test for a driver's license, answer a help-wanted advertisement, or even understand a pamphlet telling where to go for help. They experience repeated educational failures, and if they find jobs at all, they are usually temporary ones and poorly paid. And when they become parents, they are unable to prepare their children with the minimal competencies needed to succeed, so the cycle of marginal literacy and marginal living repeats.

Exercise: Level II   **N a m e :** _____
Summarizing

For a paper on indoor air pollution, summarize this passage. End your
summary with this parenthetical reference to the source: **(Nero 44-45).** It
conforms to the **MLA Documentation Style**.

Nero, Anthony V., Jr.   "Controlling Indoor Air Pollution." <u>Scientific</u>

   <u>American</u> May 1988: 42-48.

The wide range of pollutant types and concentrations entails a
correspondingly wide range of health risks. Cigarette smoke, asbestos
fibers, the decay products of radon, formaldehyde, and many other organic
chemicals are demonstrated or potential carcinogens. Most of these
pollutants can also lead to chronic or acute diseases, such as respiratory
infections and allergic responses, as can combustion products in general and
a variety of indoor bacteria and fungi. Extremely high levels of carbon
monoxide--a combustion product--can even result in immediate death. Yet
only in a relatively few cases, such as acute allergic reactions or carbon
monoxide poisoning, is there a clear-cut relation between a given exposure
to an indoor pollutant and an associated health effect. More often than not a
given instance of respiratory disease or cancer cannot be directly attributed
to a specific cause, environmental or otherwise.

Exercise: Level III   N a m e :   _____
Summary/Paraphrase
       Exercise

1.   Find an article in a magazine or professional journal that is on the
       topic of your research paper. The article should not be too long--about
       two to four pages is the right length.

2.   Photocopy the article.

3.   Write a **summary** of the entire article. You are, of course, trying to
       convey **only** the major ideas of the article; try to summarize your
       article in fewer than 150 words.

4.   Choose a short passage (one long paragraph or several short
       paragraphs) of about 150-200 words from the article. Draw a line next
       to it in the margin of your photocopy, and paraphrase just that passage.
       Here you are providing a **detailed restatement** of the passage. Your
       paraphrase will be nearly as long as, if not longer than, the original.

5.   Remember, in both versions you should strive to capture the meaning
       of the original **in your own words** (except perhaps for some key terms,
       which need not be put in quotation marks). Use your own sentence
       structures, order of information, and amount of detail. See the
       examples below for a reminder about plagiarism and key terms.

6.   Write your responses using the manuscript style specified by your
       instructor:

Remember, use your own sentence structures! Also, note the use of key terms, which are underlined in the examples.

ORIGINAL: "Morality apart, there are a number of practical reasons which form a powerful argument against capital punishment (King 374)."

WRONG: Ethics aside, there are many "practical reasons" that strongly suggest the death penalty is wrong (King 374).

ACCEPTABLE: Capital punishment is not only morally wrong; it is also impractical (King 374).

ACCEPTABLE: Capital punishment is morally wrong; perhaps more important, several practical reasons argue against it (King 374).

YOUR VERSION:

Works Cited

King, Coretta Scott. "The Death Penalty is a Step Back." Patterns Plus. Ed.

Mary Lou Conlin. 3rd ed. Boston: Houghton, 1990. 373-374.

Exercise: Level I   Name: _____

Bibliography Forms   Due: _____

DIRECTIONS: Below are bibliographic references from a paper on animal liberation. Use the forms in this book and unscramble the entries. Check the content, order, and punctuation. Alphabetize the entries.

A.   In 1977, the New York firm of Avon Books published the book <u>Animal Liberation</u>. Written by Peter Singer, the book talks of the abuse of animals and advocates vegetarianism. The book has 297 pages, 4 pages of plates, and is 18 cm. tall.

B.   On January 26, 1989, the article "Animal Rights" was published on page 13 of <u>The Christian Science Monitor</u> of Boston, Massachusetts. The author is Curtis J. Sitomer.

C.   <u>Newsweek</u> published an article by Roger Caras called "We Must Find Alternatives to Animals in Research." The article appeared on page 57 of the December 26, 1988 issue.

Exercise: Level II

Bibliography Forms

Name: _____

Due: _____

DIRECTIONS: Below are bibliographic references often by Columbus State faculty or about Columbus State. Use the entries in this book as models and write correct bibliography entries. Use only as much data as you need to complete the entry. **NOTE:** Because the entries are on different topics, you do not need to put all of the entries in alphabetical order.

1.   In 1989, Seth Hock, professor in the Computer Science Department, published the book <u>Computers and Computing</u>. The book was published by Houghton Mifflin of Boston, Massachusetts.

2.   <u>Elementary Mathematics for Computing</u> was published in 1986 by Addison-Wesley of Reading, Massachusetts. The authors are Mr. Larry R. Lance, Chairman of Columbus State's Mathematics Department, and John R. Hinton, Professor of Mathematics at Otterbein College.

3.   When the Board of Regents approved the proposal for Columbus Technical Institute to become Columbus State, <u>The Columbus Dispatch</u> reported the occasion on the first page of section B of the November 15, 1986 edition. The article's title was "CTI Transitional Move OK'd; Will Change Name to Columbus State Community College." The author is anonymous.

4.   With the change from CTI to Columbus State, the college has redesigned its mission and curriculum. The result has been fast growth. The changes at the college were reported in <u>The Columbus Dispatch</u> in an article entitled "A New Image for Columbus State." Written by Tim Doulin, the article was on page 2 B of the February 11, 1990 edition.

5.   When the Columbus Symphony hired Christian Badea, many people were apprehensive about what changes he would make. <u>Columbus Monthly</u> hired professional bassoonist and Columbus State Adjunct Faculty member Rosemary C. Hite to report on these apprehensions about the new conductor. Her article appeared on pages 141-150 of the October 1983 edition. The title is "Great Expectations at the Symphony."

6. Dr. Harold M. Nestor, president of Columbus State Community College, has been involved in technical education for many years. Suppose you have conducted an **interview** to get information about the challenges facing technical education in the year 2000. Assume that the interview was held on October 14, 1989. Write the entry.

7. On August 6, 1987, The Columbus Dispatch published a Letter to the Editor from Ithel Rook on page 16 A. In this letter Ms. Rook told of her pleasant experience coming to Columbus State as a senior citizen and of the considerate treatment she received. The letter was titled "Young People in Class Kind to Senior Citizen."

8. Columbus State has developed sports programs to promote student involvement in college activities. On pages 35-36 of the Fall 1988 issue of The Journal of the Ohio Association of Two-Year Colleges you can find the article "Strong Athletic Programs: An Important Part of a Two-Year College's Mission." The article is by Gordon Brooks of the Communication Skills Department. The issue is Volume XIV, number 1. Each issue of the journal begins with page 1.

9. You can read more about the early development of the two-year college movement in the United States by consulting the Encyclopedia of Education. In the 1971 edition, Edmund J. Gleazer, Jr. wrote the article "Growth and Status of the Junior College." The article is on pages 321-24 of Volume II. The encyclopedia is published by the Macmillan Publishing Company of New York.

Exercise:　Level III　　　　　Name:　_____

Bibliography Forms　　　　　Due:　_____

DIRECTIONS: The following sources are from a bibliography for a paper on the subject of child care in the United States. Use the models in this book and rewrite the citations in correct bibliographical format. Use only as much data as needed for a correct entry. **NOTE:** Since all of the citations are on the same topic, you must alphabetize the entries.

Article Title:	Day Care Centers
Book Title:	Encyclopedia of Education
Edition:	1st
Author:	Sadie D. Ginsberg
Editor:	Lee C. Deighton
Date:	1971
Publisher:	Crowell-Collier
Place:	New York
Page/Volume:	pages 1-6 of Volume III

Book Title:	Start Your Own At-Home Child Care Business
Edition:	1st ed.
Author:	Patricia Gallager
Date:	1989
Publisher:	Doubleday
Place:	New York
Format Notes:	305 pages; 24 cm.

Article Title:	The Day Care Dilemma
Magazine Name:	American Health
Author:	Hal Straus
Editor:	T. George Harris
Date:	September 1988
Publisher:	Owen J. Lipstein
Place:	New York
Page(s):	pages 61-65

Article Title: Pass That Child Care Bill
Newspaper
        Name: The Washington Post
Edition: morning
Author: Marian Wright Edelman
Editor: Arnold C. Graham
Date: June 20, 1989
Publisher: The Washington Post Company
Place: Washington, D. C.
Page(s):   page A 23

Article Title: Children--Abuse and Neglect
Book Title: Information Please Almanac
Edition: 43rd ed.
Author: ---
Editor: Otto Johnson
Date: 1990
Publisher: Houghton Mifflin Company
Place: Boston, Massachusetts
Page(s):   823

Article Title: In Search of Good Day Care; How to Find it
Newspaper
        Name: The Columbus Dispatch
Edition: ---
Author: ---
Editor: Luke Feck
Date: August 1, 1988
Publisher: Dispatch Printing Company
Place: Columbus, Ohio
Page(s):   3 E

Worksheet: **Writing**   **Name:**   _____

Expository Thesis & Outline   **Due:**   _____

DIRECTIONS: A.   Write a tentative thesis for your expository thesis statement. Follow the guidelines in this book or those specified by your instructor.

                                 B.   Next, write a tentative outline for your paper. As directed by your instructor, use questions, phrases, or complete sentences. Check to be sure your thesis reflects the organization you have used.

Exercise

Recognizing and Writing Issues

Name: _____

Due: _____

A   **DIRECTIONS:** Identify each of the following questions as an issue of fact, value, or policy. Then rephrase the question to illustrate least one other kind of issue.

1.   Should the nation's adoption files be opened?

2.   How adequate is the country's funding for AIDS research?

3.   Would trade sanctions against South Africa break down Apartheid?

4.   Should the United States develop a national health care system?

5.   Do intelligence tests treat minorities fairly?

6.   Does viewing pornography cause sex crimes?

7.   Can Ohio safely use its "dirty" coal?

8.   Will San Francisco suffer another major earthquake by 1995?

B.   **DIRECTIONS:** Use at least four of the following topics. For each write one issue question. Can the topics be treated logically in more than one way?

1.   steroids in sports
2.   divorce
3.   AIDS
4.   immigrants
5.   water conservation
6.   animal rights
7.   Japanese investments in U.S.
8.   greenhouse effect
9.   free-falling with a bungee cord

Worksheet

Thesis and Argumentative Outline

Name: _____

Due: _____

DIRECTIONS: As specified by your instructor, complete the following worksheet to plan your argumentative paper.

1. Write your argumentative issue, and indicate whether it is an issue of Fact, Value, or Policy.

    ----

2. If your topic is a Fact or Value, list the main Reasons you have discovered to support it.

    ----

3. If your topic is a Policy, briefly sketch the basic parts.

    Need: _____

    _____

    _____

    _____

    Plan: _____

    _____

    _____

    _____

    Practicality/Benefits: _____

    _____

    _____

    _____

4. If your issue is a Value or Policy, what objections might there be, and how might you refute them?

    Objection...   Refutation...

    _____

    _____

    _____

    _____

5. Now write a tentative opinion statement; this is the answer to your issue question. If you intend to acknowledge an opposition, indicate that at the start of your thesis; e.g., **Although it will require money and valuable space,** Columbus State should provide a child care facility.

Have this worksheet checked by your instructor before proceeding with your paper.

Exercise

Writer: _____

Peer Review

Reader: _____

DIRECTIONS: Exchange your draft with a classmate. Read each other's papers. Then provide feedback by answering the following questions.

PEER REVIEW GUIDE FOR THE RESEARCH PAPER

1. Read the opening paragraph and write a sentence below indicating what you think the paper will be about.

2. In the text, underline what you believe to be the thesis.

3. Now read the entire paper and write a sentence below indicating what the paper is actually about.

Are your answers to Questions #1 and #2 similar? If not, make some suggestions to the writer as to how to clarify the topic and purpose in the introduction.

4. Do the outline and the topic sentences match exactly? If not, mark any discrepancies. Have the changes been made for stylistic reasons? _____ Yes _____ No

5. Does the introduction have an attention-getting device? _____ Yes _____ No

6. Does the conclusion do more than summarize? _____ Yes _____ No

7. Do all topic sentences help support the thesis? _____ Yes _____ No

8. Does the student use the following? (Check if used)

_____ in-text quotations   _____ blocked quotations   _____ summary/paraphrase

_____ in-line quote   _____ at least five parenthetical references

9. Does all borrowed material begin with a lead-in device? If not, indicate where leads should be written.   _____ Yes _____ No

10. Does all borrowed material end with a parenthetical reference device? If not, indicate where changes or additions need to be made.   _____ Yes _____ No

11. Are the lead-ins varied? appropriate? helpful? If not, indicate where changes or additions need to be made.   _____ Yes _____ No

12. Does the student avoid using contractions?   _____ Yes _____ No

13. Are sources on the Works cited page formatted correctly?   _____ Yes _____ No

Does the student use at least two different types of sources?   _____ Yes _____ No

Are they arranged in alphabetical order?   _____ Yes _____ No

14. Are the pages numbered correctly?   _____ Yes _____ No

15. Is the title page correct?   _____ Yes _____ No

16. Is there an outline page? Note any errors.   _____ Yes _____ No

17. Is the paper of sufficient length? (5 to 7 pages)   _____ Yes _____ No

18. Has the student written correct and effective sentences? If not, mark what you believe to be errors.   _____ Yes _____ No

19. Mark what you believe to be spelling errors. (sp)

20. Mark what you believe to be punctuation errors. (p)

Exercise

Oral Presentation

Name: _____

Due: _____

DIRECTIONS: Prepare and deliver a presentation that reports on your research, your findings, and your final thoughts about your essay--unless otherwise directed, answer the following questions. The time limit for this report should be 5-7 minutes.

1. Define your specific topic or issue.

2. Summarize the main points of your development.

3. Discuss the impact of your research and writing on your opinion. Has it intensified? Altered? Explain.

4. Briefly discuss what sources of material you found most useful for your research and writing.

Acknowledgments

Robert Kaldenbach: From "Starting Your Own Little Country Inn," Yankee Magazine, Copyright (c) 1984 by Yankee Publishing Inc.

Jan Stankus: From How to Open and Operate a Bed and Breakfast Home by Jan Stankus. Copyright (c) 1986 by Globe Pequot.